Another Sunrise In Kentucky

More Recipes From Kentucky's Finest Bed & Breakfast Inns

Tracy & Phyllis Winters

Winters Publishing
P.O. Box 501
Greensburg, Indiana 47240

800-457-3230
812-663-4948

© 1997 Tracy Winters
All rights reserved
Printed in the United States of America

Cover photo by: Faith Echtermeyer
Courtesy of: Mark & Christi Carter

The information about the inns and the recipes were supplied by the inns themselves. The rate information was current at the time of submission, but is subject to change. Every effort has been made to assure that the book is accurate. Neither the Bed & Breakfast Association of Kentucky, the individual inns or the publisher assume responsibility for any errors, whether typographical or otherwise.

Library of Congress Card Catalog Number 97-90381
ISBN 1-883651-06-9

Preface

We trust that you will enjoy sampling some of the recipes in this copy of *Another Sunrise In Kentucky*. We also invite you to take a journey to some of the fine Kentucky inns which are included.

We have endeavored to provide you with an error-free cookbook, and although the recipes included have been tested at each of the Bed and Breakfasts, they were not specifically tested for this cookbook. These recipes represent some of the personal favorites of the innkeepers, and we are proud to bring them to you.

We hope that you enjoy *Another Sunrise In Kentucky*. Please visit some of the inns featured inside and enjoy warm hospitality and delicious food.

Rates

We have used the following symbols to represent the price range of the Bed & Breakfast Inns:

$ - $50 or less
$$ - $51 to $75
$$$ - $76 to $100
$$$$ - more than $100

Please call ahead to verify rates and room availability.

CONTENTS

A TRUE INN Bed & Breakfast 6

Aleksander House 8

Alpine Lodge 10

Augusta White House Inn Bed & Breakfast 12

Barnes Mill Bed & Breakfast 14

Bauer Haus Bed & Breakfast 16

Baxter House 20

Beautiful Dreamer Bed & Breakfast 22

Bourbon House Farm 24

The Brand House at Rose Hill 26

Cedar Haven Farm Bed & Breakfast 28

Cedar Rock Farm 32

Cliffview Resort 34

College Street Inn 36

Ghent House Bed & Breakfast 38

Glenmar Plantation Bed & Breakfast 40

Helton House Bed & Breakfast 42

Inn at the Park Bed & Breakfast 44

L & N Bed & Breakfast 46

Lafayette Heights Clubhouse 48

Licking Riverside Historic Bed & Breakfast 50

Maple Hill Manor Bed & Breakfast 52

The Marcum-Porter House Bed & Breakfast 56

Myers' Bed & Breakfast 58

Myrtledene Bed & Breakfast	60
Old Louisville Inn Bed & Breakfast	62
Old Talbott Tavern / McLean House	64
The Oldham House Bed & Breakfast and Antiques	66
Osbornes of Cabin Hollow	68
Pineapple Inn Bed & Breakfast	70
Randolph House	72
The Ridgerunner Bed & Breakfast	74
Rocking Horse Manor Bed & Breakfast	76
Rose Blossom Bed & Breakfast	78
Rosedale Bed & Breakfast	80
Sandford House Bed & Breakfast	84
Sandusky House & O'Neal Log Cabin	86
Seldon Renaker Inn	90
Sills Inn Bed & Breakfast	92
Silver Cliff Inn Bed & Breakfast	94
Susan B. Seay's Magnolia Manor	96
Trinity Hills Farm Bed & Breakfast Home	98
Victorian House Bed & Breakfast	100
The Wayfarer	102
Weller Haus Bed & Breakfast	104
Willis Graves 1830's Bed & Breakfast Inn	106
Woodhaven Bed & Breakfast	108
Order Form	111
Index Of Inns	112

A TRUE INN Bed & Breakfast

467 West Second Street • Lexington, KY 40507
606-252-6166
Innkeepers: Beverly & Bobby True

Newly renovated 1843 Victorian Elegance in heart of Historic Downtown, is on the National Register and Bluegrass Trust. Spacious formal rooms and gardens. All rooms are beautifully decorated with antique furnishings. Five bedrooms, private baths, one has double jacuzzi. Full breakfast, carriage tours - walk to all major attractions, shops, and dining.

Rates: $$$ - $$$$ Includes full breakfast. Children over age 10 are welcome. No pets, please. Restricted smoking. We accept MasterCard, Visa, Am Ex, and Discover.

Recipes From A TRUE INN Bed & Breakfast

CHERRY COFFEE CAKE

1 pound loaf frozen bread dough, thawed
1 can cherry pie filling
1/2 cup all-purpose flour
Glaze:
1 cup confectioner's sugar
1/3 cup sugar
1/3 cup cold butter or margarine
1/4 teaspoon vanilla

3 tablespoons milk

Roll dough into a lightly greased 13 1/4" pizza pan. Bake at 350° for 5 minutes. Pour cherry pie filling over dough. Combine flour and sugar in small bowl; cut in butter and vanilla until crumbly. Sprinkle over pie filling. Bake at 350° for 25 to 30 minutes or until edges are golden brown. Cool. Combine glaze ingredients in small bowl and drizzle over coffee cake.

FRIED POTATO CAKES

4 cups frozen shredded potatoes
2 eggs, lightly beaten
1/2 cup chopped onion
1/3 cup all-purpose flour
3 tablespoons minced fresh parsley
1 teaspoon salt
1 teaspoon pepper

Rinse potatoes in cold water, drain thoroughly. In a bowl, mix potatoes, eggs, onion, flour, parsley, salt, and pepper. Pour batter by 1/3 cupfuls onto a greased hot griddle. Fry on each side until golden brown. Makes 10 potato pancakes.

Aleksander House

1213 South First Street • Louisville, KY 40203
502-637-4985
Innkeeper: Nancy Hinchliff

Built in 1882, the **Aleksander House** is a spacious, Victorian Italianate home located in Old Louisville. Listed in the National Registry of Historic Landmarks, the three-story home features 12-foot ceilings, original hardwood floors, moldings, staircases, and five fireplaces. Four guest rooms are tastefully decorated in an eclectic blend of period and contemporary furnishings, including modern baths, telephones, television, and air-conditioning. Some have VCR's and computer and fax machine hook-ups. **Aleksander House** is conveniently located just minutes from downtown Louisville, Churchill Downs, the airport, and many fine eating establishments. Open all year-round, **Aleksander House** offers spacious, comfortable rooms and sumptuous gourmet breakfasts: from Southern scratch biscuits, grits, and sausage to Dutch-oven German pancakes smothered in warm cinnamon apples. Specially blended coffees, fine teas, homemade granolas, muffins, jams, & butters complete their gourmet fare. They will be happy to prepare heart-healthy meals tailored to your needs.

Rates: $$ - $$$ Includes full breakfast. Children over age 12 are welcome. No pets, please. Restricted smoking. We accept MasterCard and Visa.

Recipes From Aleksander House

ALEK'S RASPBERRY MUFFINS

1/2 cup (1 stick) butter (room temperature)
3/4 cup sugar
2 eggs
1 1/2 cups flour
1 teaspoon salt
1 teaspoon baking soda
1/2 teaspoon nutmeg
1/4 teaspoon allspice
1/4 teaspoon ground cloves
3/4 cup sour cream
1 1/2 cups fresh or partially frozen raspberries (do not defrost completely)
1 teaspoon vanilla

Preheat oven to 350°. Line 18 muffin cups with paper muffin liners. Cream butter and sugar until light and fluffy. Add eggs and beat well. In another bowl, sift dry ingredients together. Add to butter mixture; combine well. Add sour cream, fresh or partially frozen raspberries, and vanilla. Mix carefully until just blended. Fill muffin cups 3/4 full. Sprinkle tops of muffins with granulated sugar. Bake 20 to 30 minutes. Test with toothpick. When it comes out dry, muffins are done. Cool 5 minutes. Turn out of muffin tins onto rack. *Dough can be frozen in muffin tins and kept in freezer for several weeks. Bake frozen dough at 350° for 30 minutes. Makes 18 muffins.

TOMATO-ONION QUICHE

1 unbaked 9" pie shell
3/4 cup shredded mozzarella cheese
3/4 cup shredded Cheddar cheese
1/2 cup shredded Swiss cheese
3 medium tomatoes, peeled & sliced thinly
1/2 cup onions, peeled & sliced thinly
Salt and cracked pepper, to taste
1 teaspoon dried basil
1 teaspoon garlic powder
2 eggs
3/4 cup half and half
3 tablespoons grated Parmesan cheese

Preheat oven to 350°. Line 9" pie or quiche pan with unbaked pie dough (shell). Sprinkle shredded cheeses on bottom of unbaked pie shell. Layer tomatoes and onions over cheese. Sprinkle salt, cracked pepper, basil, and garlic powder over cheese. Beat eggs and half and half together and pour over tomatoes and onions. Sprinkle Parmesan cheese on top. Bake at 350° for 45 to 50 minutes or until set. *Quiche can be prepared the night before and refrigerated. Do not bake pie shell ahead. Bake next day at 350° for 45 to 50 minutes.

Alpine Lodge

5310 Morgantown Road • Bowling Green, KY 42101-8201
502-843-4846
Innkeepers: Dr. & Mrs. David Livingston

Alpine Lodge is a Swiss chalet with 6,000 square feet. It has a honeymoon suite, a family suite that sleeps five, a king, and a double. There is a swimming pool and hot tub. We have 12 acres of trails for hiking. We serve a full country breakfast of biscuits and gravy, fried apples, eggs, grits, coffee, and orange juice.

Rates: $ - $$$ Includes full breakfast. Children are welcome. Pets allowed. Restricted smoking.

Recipes From Alpine Lodge

BREAKFAST PIZZA

1 pound pork sausage
1 pkg. refrigerated crescent rolls
1 cup shredded Colby & Monterey Jack cheeses
5 eggs
1/4 cup milk
Salt & pepper, to taste
2 tablespoons Parmesan cheese

Cook sausage and drain grease. Spread crescent rolls over bottom of pizza pan, pat out to cover entire pan. Spoon drained sausage over crust. Top with shredded cheese. In bowl beat eggs with milk, salt, and pepper. Pour over cheese. Sprinkle with Parmesan cheese. Bake at 350° for 25 to 30 minutes. Makes 6 - 8 servings.

QUICK ROLLS

2 cups Bisquick baking mix
1 cup sour cream
1 stick margarine, melted

Melt margarine, and mix all ingredients together. Bake in greased muffin tins at 450° for 15 minutes. Makes 6 - 8 servings.

Augusta White House Inn Bed & Breakfast

307 Main Street • Augusta, KY 41002-1038
606-756-2004
Innkeepers: R. C. Spencer and J. J. Spencer

The Augusta White House Inn B&B is located in the heart of historic Augusta, one of the few remaining Ohio river towns without a flood wall to obstruct the river view. **The Inn**, housed in a restored, circa 1830 Victorian brick, "The John Buerger Tin Shop", is on the National Registry and designated a Kentucky Landmark. The interior, with flowered wallpapers and high crown-molded ceilings, retains the elegance and style of the very early Victorian era. Comfortably sized rooms are all updated with modern conveniences such as air conditioning. In addition to their own room, guests have use of the parlor and 6' grand piano, formal dining room, living room with an abundance of reading materials, and cable television. Smokers are made welcome on the sheltered front porch. Breakfast includes an array of gourmet entrees and side dishes to please even the most discriminating palate.

Rates: $ - $$$ Includes full breakfast. Children over age 12 are welcome. No pets or smoking, please. We accept MasterCard, Visa, Am Ex, and Discover.

Recipes From Augusta White House Inn B & B

CHEESE POPOVERS

2 large eggs
1 cup plus 2 teaspoons all-purpose flour
1 cup half and half
2 teaspoons melted butter
1/8 teaspoon salt
1 1/2 ounces grated Parmesan cheese

Preheat oven to 375°. Spray eight 4-ounce muffin tins with non-stick cooking spray. In bowl, beat eggs, then beat in flour, half and half, butter, and salt until blended. Stir in cheese. Place batter in tin and bake for 35 to 40 minutes until puffed and golden. Serve hot. Makes 4 servings.

FOUR CHEESE/THREE ONION PIE

<u>Crust:</u>
1 cup all-purpose flour
2 tablespoons whole wheat flour
1/8 teaspoon salt

<u>Filling:</u>
1/4 cup chicken broth
1 cup chopped onion (not sweet onion)
3/4 cup sliced white part of leek
1/4 cup sliced scallions
1 cup half and half
2 large eggs
2 teaspoons arrowroot
1/2 teaspoon dried basil
1/8 teaspoon salt

1/8 teaspoon black pepper
1/4 cup butter, chilled
2 tablespoons ice water, more or less

1/8 teaspoon black pepper
Pinch of ground red pepper
2 ounces shredded Cheddar cheese
2 ounces shredded Swiss cheese
2 ounces shredded Monterey Jack cheese
2 tablespoons grated Parmesan cheese

Combine first four crust ingredients. Cut in butter until coarse crumbs are formed. Stir in ice water one tablespoon at a time until mixture becomes a cohesive dough. Gather dough into ball, seal in container and refrigerate for 30 minutes. Preheat oven to 375°. For Filling: Warm broth in skillet over medium heat. Add onion, leek, and scallions and sauté until transparent; set aside. Blend half and half, eggs, and seasonings. Roll chilled dough between non-stick sheets to an 11' circle - fit into 9" pie plate, prick shell bottom and trim overhang, leaving enough dough to make decorative edge with thumbs or fork. Bake for 10 minutes while keeping crust flat with weights. Remove from oven and brush with egg-milk mixture. Bake a few more minutes until dry, remove and cool. Sprinkle onions and cheeses evenly into shell. Pour egg-milk mixture over shell. Bake until golden brown and puffed. Makes 6 servings.

Barnes Mill Bed & Breakfast

1268 Barnes Mill Road • Richmond, KY 40475
606-623-5509
Innkeepers: Christine and Euzenith Sowers

Barnes Mill Bed & Breakfast, located only one-half mile from I-75 - 876 W, Richmond, is surrounded by a picturesque farm of black fences, grazing cattle, and rolling hills. Built in 1916, the house has been completely renovated and restored to its Victorian elegance and Old South charm. We are located half-way between Lexington and Berea in the beautiful "Bluegrass of Kentucky". Close by you will find Bybee Pottery, Boonesborough, Whitehall, and Gibson Bay Golf Course. Enjoy the large spacious house and big porches. A full country breakfast is served. Homemade bread a specialty! Enjoy true Southern hospitality.

Rates: $$ Includes full breakfast. Children are welcome. No pets, please. Restricted smoking. We accept MasterCard and Visa.

Recipes From Barnes Mill Bed & Breakfast

CREAM CHEESE COFFEE CAKE

3 sticks butter, softened
8 ounces cream cheese, softened
3 cups sugar
6 whole eggs
1 1/2 teaspoons vanilla
3 cups flour
1/4 teaspoon salt

Preheat oven to 325°. Beat butter and cream cheese together. Add sugar - beat until light and fluffy. Add eggs one at a time, beating well. Add vanilla, flour, and salt. Spoon into well-greased cake mold and bake for one hour and 15 minutes or until it tests done. Cool 5 minutes in pan before turning out on plate. Dust with confectioner's sugar if desired.

EASY SCRAMBLED EGGS

1 tablespoon oil
2 tablespoons chopped green pepper
2 tablespoons chopped celery
1 teaspoon flour
1/4 cup milk
6 eggs, beaten
Salt and pepper, to taste

Heat oil in skillet, add chopped green pepper, and celery. Cook about three minutes. Combine flour, milk, and eggs. Add to skillet and cook until done. *Cooked diced or chopped ham may be added if desired. An easy and tasty dish!

Bauer Haus Bed & Breakfast

362 North College Street • Harrodsburg, KY 40330
606-734-6289
Innkeepers: Dick and Marian Bauer

The Bauer Haus is a lovely 1880's Victorian home on the National Register of Historic Places, in an historic district of Kentucky's oldest settlement. Enter the 8' 5" front door into the large main hall. Nestle in the sitting room, sip tea or coffee in the dining room, repose in the parlor, or ascend the staircase to one of four spacious guest rooms for a relaxing visit. Stresses dissipate on the inset front porch with Tuscan columns, where a double swing or wicker furniture invite relaxation, weather permitting. For a getaway to a bygone era, **Bauer Haus** offers the ultimate opportunity. Walk to Old Fort Harrod or historic downtown with unique shops & antique malls. A short drive away, Shaker Village at Pleasant Hill offers a variety of programs and activities reflecting the simpler life of the Shakers, while the *Dixie Belle* paddle wheel provides a leisurely ride on the Kentucky River.

Rates: $$ Includes full breakfast. No pets, please. Restricted smoking. We accept MasterCard and Visa.

Recipes From Bauer Haus Bed & Breakfast

BAKED FRUIT COMPOTE

16 ounce can dark pitted sweet cherries, drained
1/2 cup firmly packed brown sugar
1 tablespoon cornstarch
2 1/2 tablespoons lemon juice
1/4 cup orange juice
29 ounce can sliced peaches, drained
6 ounces dried apricots
6 ounces pitted prunes
1 tablespoon cherry brandy

Drain cherries and reserve liquid. Set aside. Combine brown sugar and cornstarch. Gradually add cherry juice, lemon juice, and orange juice. Stir mixture well. Combine cherries, peaches, apricots, and prunes in a 2-quart casserole. Pour brown sugar mixture over fruit. Sprinkle with cherry brandy. Cover and bake at 350° for 45 minutes or until apricots are tender. Serve warm or at room temperature. Makes 10 - 12 servings.

LOW-FAT CINNAMON BREAKFAST CAKE

3/4 cup sugar
4 tablespoons applesauce (or 4 tablespoons butter)
1 egg substitute (or 1 egg)
Streusel:
1/2 cup brown sugar
2 tablespoons flour
1/2 cup skim milk
1 1/2 cups flour
2 teaspoons baking powder
1/2 teaspoon salt

2 teaspoons cinnamon
2 tablespoons butter

Mix together sugar, applesauce, and egg substitute. Stir in milk. Add flour, baking powder, and salt. Stir until smooth. Spread half the batter in 9" pan sprayed with Pam. Add half the streusel mix over the batter. Pour on remainder of batter and top with other half of streusel. Bake about 25 to 30 minutes. Serve warm from oven. *May peel and slice one Granny Smith apple thinly between batter on bottom and streusel. Makes 6 - 8 servings.

Recipes From Bauer Haus Bed & Breakfast

BANANA-ORANGE MUFFINS

2 cups flour
1 teaspoon baking soda
1 teaspoon baking powder
1 1/2 teaspoons pumpkin pie spice (or 3/4 teaspoon cinnamon, 1/4 teaspoon cloves, 1/4 teaspoon nutmeg, and 1/4 teaspoon ginger)
1 cup mashed bananas (3 ripe bananas)
6 ounces orange juice
2 eggs (or egg substitute)
2 tablespoons margarine (or 2 tablespoons applesauce)
1 cup raisins
1 cup chopped nuts (opt.)

In large mixing bowl, place first four ingredients. In small mixing bowl, mix together bananas, orange juice, eggs, and margarine or applesauce. Add this to flour mixture. Add raisins and nuts (if desired). Mix together well. Spray muffin tins with non-stick spray. Fill 3/4 full. Bake at 350° for 15 to 20 minutes. Makes 18 muffins.

GINGER-OAT CAKES

1 1/2 cups skim milk
3/4 cup quick-cooking oats
1 cup all-purpose flour
1 1/2 teaspoons baking powder
1 teaspoon ground cinnamon
1/2 teaspoon ground ginger
1/4 teaspoon baking soda
1 egg substitute
3 egg whites, beaten
2 tablespoons applesauce
2 tablespoons molasses

In small saucepan, heat milk over low heat just until hot. Stir in oats. Remove from heat and let stand 5 minutes. In medium mixing bowl put dry ingredients together. Stir in cooked oats just until moistened. In separate bowl combine egg substitute, egg whites, applesauce, and molasses. Stir in oat mixture. For each pancake, pour about 1/4 cup batter onto hot nonstick skillet sprayed with non-stick spray. Cook until light golden brown. Turn to cook other side when surface is bubbly and edges are slightly dry. Eat pancakes plain or top with fresh or spreadable fruit. *Can add 1 cup blueberries to batter. Prepared batter can be refrigerated for up to 2 days. Makes 14 - 3 1/2" pancakes.

Recipes From Bauer Haus Bed & Breakfast

HASH BROWN & SAUSAGE MINI-FRITTATAS

1/4 pound spicy turkey sausage (1/2 cup)
1 teaspoon canola oil (or spray)
1 small onion, chopped (1/2 cup)
1 1/2 cups frozen hash brown potatoes, thawed
1 clove garlic, very finely chopped, or 1/2 teaspoon garlic powder
1 teaspoon dried oregano
1 teaspoon dried thyme
1/2 teaspoon salt
1/2 teaspoon freshly ground black pepper
1/3 cup water
3 large eggs
2 large egg whites
1 cup non-fat buttermilk
1/4 cup freshly grated Parmesan cheese
2 tablespoons all-purpose white flour
1 cup prepared salsa

Preheat oven to 350°. Spray 12 muffin cups with non-stick cooking spray; set aside. Spray skillet with cooking spray, heat over medium-high heat. Crumble sausage into pan and cook until browned, about 5 minutes, while stirring. Remove sausage. In skillet heat oil (or add more spray); add onions & potatoes; cook until light golden, about 10 minutes. Stir occasionally. Stir in garlic, oregano, thyme, salt, and pepper, & browned sausage. Cook while stirring for 1 minute more. Add water and stir until water has just evaporated, about 1 minute. Remove from heat. In bowl, whisk eggs, egg whites, buttermilk, Parmesan, & flour. Add sausage and vegetables. Spoon mixture into prepared muffin cups. Bake about 20 minutes until set and golden on top. Run small knife around the edges to loosen. Serve immediately, passing salsa alongside. Makes about 12 mini-frittatas for 4.

Baxter House

1677 Lexington Road • Harrodsburg, KY 40330
606-734-5700
Innkeeper: Jack Leonard

Baxter House, in historic Harrodsburg, has been returned to its original turn-of-the-century comfort, and updated with its proprietor's personal taste that has become its signature. The walls of one of four spacious guest rooms (each with private bath) are awash with a warm, welcoming salmon color. Overstuffed easy chairs encourage you to curl up with a favorite book after a full day of exploring Kentucky's heartland, and handmade quilts invite you to nestle in your comfortable antique bed. Plan your own itinerary to explore central Kentucky, or be directed to antiques, arts and crafts, Shakertown at Pleasant Hill, Old Fort Harrod, or nearby Perryville Battlefield, of interest to Civil War buffs. It's just a quick trot to magnificent Bluegrass country to visit the Kentucky Horse Farm, or ride a nearby mount. Come for a getaway, and you will return again and again!

Rates: $$$ Includes continental plus breakfast. No pets, please. Restricted smoking.

Recipes From Baxter House

GRANNY BENNETT'S OATMEAL MUFFINS

1 cup uncooked oatmeal
1 cup buttermilk
1 egg
1/2 cup brown sugar
1/2 cup oil
1 cup flour
1 teaspoon baking powder
1/2 teaspoon salt
1/2 teaspoon baking soda
1/2 cup raisins or chopped dates

Mix oatmeal and buttermilk in large bowl. Let set 1 hour. Add egg, brown sugar, and oil. In small bowl, combine flour, baking powder, salt, and baking soda. Mix all together and add raisins or dates. Bake at 350° for 20 minutes. Makes 12 muffins. *2 egg whites and 1/2 cup applesauce can replace oil and whole egg to reduce fat content.

LEMON GROVE WALNUT MUFFINS

1 cup sugar
1/2 cup (1 stick) softened sweet butter
2 eggs
1 cup unflavored yogurt
2 teaspoons grated lemon peel
1 1/2 cups coarsely chopped walnuts
1 teaspoon baking soda
2 cups flour

Cream sugar and butter; add eggs one at a time, then yogurt, lemon peel, walnuts, and baking soda. Add flour gradually, mixing until well-blended. Spoon into greased or paper-lined muffin tins. Bake at 375° for 18 to 20 minutes. Makes 12 large muffins.

Beautiful Dreamer Bed & Breakfast

440 East Stephen Foster Avenue • Bardstown, KY 40004
502-348-4004   800-811-8312
Innkeeper: Lynell Ginter

Located in Bardstown Historic District, our Federal-design home (circa 1995), is complemented with antiques and cherry furniture. Relax on our porches and enjoy a breathtaking view of My Old Kentucky Home. You can show off your talent on our baby grand piano, and no matter what room you're staying in, you'll enjoy our central air. Stay in our Beautiful Dreamer room where you'll forget all your worries in our double jacuzzi. This is the perfect room for special occasions. Our Captain's room has a beautiful fireplace, and a single jacuzzi. The Stephen Foster room is handicapped accessible. All our rooms have queen-sized beds and private baths. A hearty breakfast is included. Don't worry about getting stuck in traffic on your way to The Stephen Foster Story - you can just walk there. Come, make your own beautiful dreams in our **Beautiful Dreamer Bed & Breakfast.**

Rates: $$$ Includes full breakfast. Children over age 8 are welcome. No pets or smoking, please. We accept MasterCard and Visa.

Recipes From Beautiful Dreamer Bed & Breakfast

SCRAMBLED EGG CASSEROLE

Cheese Sauce:
2 tablespoons butter
2 1/2 tablespoons flour
2 cups milk
1/2 teaspoon salt
1/8 teaspoon ground pepper
1 cup shredded American cheese

1 cup cubed ham
1/4 cup chopped green onion
3 tablespoons melted butter
1 dozen eggs, beaten

Topping:
1/4 cup melted butter
2 1/4 cups soft bread crumbs

For Cheese Sauce: Melt butter, blend in flour, and cook for 1 minute. Gradually stir in milk; cook until thick. Add salt, pepper and cheese; stir until cheese melts. Set aside. Sauté ham and green onions in 3 tablespoons melted butter until onions are tender. Add eggs, and cook over medium heat until eggs are set. Stir in the Cheese Sauce; pour into greased 9" x 13" x 2" baking pan. Combine topping ingredients, spread evenly over egg mixture. Cover, chill overnight. Uncover and bake at 350° for 30 minutes. Makes 10 - 12 servings.

SORGHUM PEACHES

Canned peach halves
1/2 teaspoon sorghum molasses (per peach)

1/2 teaspoon butter (per peach)
Cinnamon, to taste (opt.)

Place the desired number of peaches, pitted side up, in a shallow buttered baking dish. Put sorghum and butter in each peach half; allow some sorghum to fall around the dish. Bake at 350° for 15 minutes. Serve hot. *Brown sugar may be used instead of sorghum. For variation, an assortment of fruits (peaches, pears, and apricots) is good. Cinnamon may be lightly sprinkled on top before baking.

Bourbon House Farm

584 Shropshire Lane • Georgetown, KY 40324
606-987-8669
Innkeepers: Peter VanAndel and Lynn Lewis

Bourbon House is a charming 1820 country manor house and horse farm, perfect for relaxing and as a central point for exploring the Bluegrass area. There is a one-half mile tree-lined lane leading up to the house that sits on a hill, commanding a view of geometric paddocks, rolling hills, and a patchwork of open fields. Offered to guests are two large and lovely bedrooms with sitting areas, king-sized beds, additional sleeping capability, and ensuite baths. A complete breakfast is served in the formal dining room or the screened-in morning porch. Long walks, fishing, biking, croquet, naps on the porch, or in the hammock, are all available. Convenient to Bluegrass attractions and University of Kentucky.

Rates: $$$ Includes full breakfast. Children over age 11 are welcome. No pets, please. Restricted smoking. We accept MasterCard and Visa.

Recipes From Bourbon House Farm

BOURBON HOUSE FARM GRANOLA

8 cups rolled oats
1 1/2 cups packed brown sugar
1 1/2 cups regular wheat germ
8 ounces shredded coconut

1 1/2 cups hulled sunflower seeds
1/2 cup sliced almonds
3/4 cup honey
2 teaspoons vanilla
1/2 cup canola oil
Fresh berries

Blend oats, sugar, wheat germ, coconut, seeds, and almonds. Heat honey, vanilla, and oil in cooking pot, stirring until mixture boils. Mix liquids with dry mixture. Lightly grease 2 - 1 quart baking pans and spread granola evenly between pans. Bake at 325° for approximately 20 minutes until coconut is lightly browned, stirring several times. After removing from oven, stir occasionally to cool. Serve with milk and berries. Makes 12 - 16 servings.

FINNISH PANCAKE WITH FRUIT COMPOTE

4 eggs
1/4 cup honey
3/4 teaspoon salt
2 1/2 cups milk

1 cup all-purpose flour
2 tablespoons butter, melted

<u>Fruit Topping:</u>
1 1/2 cups raspberries

1/4 cup orange juice
1 cup blueberries

Preheat oven to 400°. For pancake: Beat eggs, honey, salt, and milk in large bowl. Add flour and mix until blended. Melt butter, and pour into Teflon bundt pan. Pour in batter and bake for 25 minutes. Invert onto serving plate. Serve at once with Fruit Topping. For Topping: Purée 3 tablespoons raspberries and orange juice. Place in medium cooking pot and heat. Remove from heat and add remaining fruit. Pour over pancake. Makes 6 servings.

The Brand House at Rose Hill

461 North Limestone Street • Lexington, KY 40508
606-226-9464   800-366-4942
Innkeepers: Pam and Logan Leet

In 1802, John Brand traveled from his native Scotland to America, rebuilding his hemp business in Lexington. He prospered, and built his home, "Rose Hill", in 1812 in the heart of today's downtown Lexington. The Federal one-story home continues to be a significant example of Antebellum architecture, has been featured in Southern Living and National Geographic magazines, and is listed on the National Register of Historic Places. In 1994, **The Brand House** was purchased by the present owners who totally renovated the property as a B&B. The five rooms have been restored to retain their original ambiance, while adding the contemporary conveniences today's travelers expect. The professionally decorated rooms all have private attached baths with whirlpool tubs. Common areas include the formal dining room, elegant drawing room, and billiard room. Tariff includes a full, gourmet breakfast and social hour in the afternoon.

Rates: $$$ - $$$$ Includes full breakfast. Children over age 12 are welcome. No pets, please. Restricted smoking. We accept MasterCard, Visa, Am Ex, and Discover.

Recipes From The Brand House at Rose Hill

BLUEBERRY MOUSSE

2 envelopes unflavored
  gelatin
1/4 cup cold water
1 pint blueberries

2 cups heavy cream
4 egg whites (or
  substitute*)
2 cups sugar

Sprinkle gelatin over cold water in small saucepan. Stir over low heat just until dissolved. Set aside to cool. Wash berries and purée in blender or food processor. Add gelatin. Beat cream until soft peaks form, then gradually add 1 cup sugar. Beat egg whites until fluffy, then add remaining sugar. *Due to concern about raw eggs, substitute Meringue Powder, purchased in most groceries or specialty cake departments, to the equivalent of 4 egg whites. Fold together all ingredients. Chill overnight and garnish with whole berries.

CHEESE GRITS FLORENTINE

2 cloves garlic
2 teaspoons olive oil
6 ounces country or city
  ham, diced
4 1/2 cups chicken or
  vegetable broth
1 1/2 cups quick-cooking
  grits
1/2 cup butter
1/2 - 1 teaspoon salt

1 teaspoon white
  pepper
1 - 1 1/2 cups half
  and half
6 eggs
2 cups grated Swiss
  cheese
10 ounces frozen,
  chopped spinach,
  thawed & drained

Sauté garlic cloves in olive oil in skillet over medium heat. Add ham just until browned; set aside. Cook grits according to package directions, substituting broth for water. When grits are thick, remove from heat and add butter. Combine salt, pepper, half and half, and eggs in mixing bowl and beat until well blended. Add ham, egg mixture, Swiss cheese, & spinach to grits. Blend thoroughly. Grease 9" x 12" casserole dish, quiche pan or individual ramekins. Spoon grits into baking dish. Bake at 350° for 35 to 45 minutes until firm and bubbly. Sprinkle with additional cheese before serving if desired.

Cedar Haven Farm Bed & Breakfast

2380 Bethel Road • Nicholasville, KY 40356
606-858-3849
Innkeepers: Irene and Jim Smith

You can enjoy the quiet, relaxed atmosphere at our farm home B&B. Sitting in a rocking chair on the front porch in the evening, listening to the night sounds, watching the fireflies, one can forget life in the fast lane and gain a whole new perspective. We provide three guest rooms. The full country breakfast served each morning will energize you for a full day's activities, exploring the multitude of exciting things to do in the Bluegrass area of Central Kentucky.

Rates: $ Includes full breakfast. Children are welcome. Pets are allowed with prior permission. No smoking, please.

ALL-BRAN ROLLS

1 cup All-Bran
1/2 cup sugar
1 1/2 teaspoons salt
1 cup lard (or oil or Crisco)
1 cup boiling water

1 cup lukewarm water
2 packages dry yeast
2 eggs
6 cups all-purpose flour, sifted

Pour boiling water over first 4 combined items. Mix well until lard is melted and mixture is cool. Dissolve yeast in warm water, set aside. Add eggs to All-Bran mixture and beat slightly with hand rotary beater. Add yeast mixture and mix well. Add flour and mix well. Refrigerate overnight. Roll out 1/2" thick and cut out with biscuit cutter. Let rise 2 1/2 to 3 hours. Bake in preheated 400° oven approximately 15 minutes. Makes 3 - 3 1/2 dozen rolls.

ALMOND-HONEY GRANOLA

4 cups rolled oats
1 1/2 cups almonds
1 cup wheat germ

1/2 cup coconut
1/2 cup honey
1/2 cup vegetable oil

Toss all ingredients together. Turn into large shallow pan. Bake at 350° for 30 minutes, stirring occasionally. Break up lumps. Store in an airtight container. Makes 2 quarts.

Recipes From Cedar Haven Farm Bed & Breakfast

BAKED PEACH HALVES

3 tablespoons brown sugar
3/4 teaspoon freshly ground ginger
3/4 teaspoon grated lemon rind
2 - 16 ounce cans peach halves, drained

Combine first three ingredients, sprinkle evenly over top of each peach half. Bake at 375° for 8 to 10 minutes or until thoroughly heated. Serve hot. *Freshly ground nutmeg can be used instead of ginger, according to taste. Makes 6 servings.

STRAWBERRY COFFEE CAKE

3 ounces cream cheese
1/4 cup butter
2 cups biscuit mix
1/3 cup milk
1/2 cup strawberry jam

Cut cream cheese and butter into biscuit mix until crumbly. Blend in milk. Turn out onto a slightly floured surface; knead 8 to 10 strokes. On waxed paper, roll dough to a 12" x 8" rectangle. Turn onto greased baking sheet; remove waxed paper. Spread strawberry jam down center of dough. Make 2 - 1/2" cuts at 1" intervals on long sides. Fold strips over filling. Bake at 425° for 12 to 15 minutes. Drizzle coffee cake with icing. Makes approximately 8 servings.

Recipes From Cedar Haven Farm Bed & Breakfast

BLUEBERRY SAUCE

2 cups fresh blueberries
1/3 cup orange juice
2 tablespoons sugar

2 teaspoons cornstarch
Pinch of ground nutmeg

Combine all ingredients in saucepan. Cook over medium heat for four to five minutes until thickened, stirring continuously. Great with pancakes! Makes approximately 2 1/2 cups.

STRAWBERRY SCONES

2 cups plain flour
3 tablespoons sugar, divided
1 tablespoon baking powder

1/2 teaspoon salt
1/4 cup margarine, cut up
2/3 cup milk
1 large egg, beaten
1/3 cup strawberry jam

Preheat oven to 425°. Grease cookie sheet. In large bowl combine flour, 2 tablespoons sugar, baking powder, and salt. Cut in butter with pastry blender until like coarse crumbs. Stir in milk, and egg, just until combined. Turn dough out on lightly floured surface; knead about 4 times until dough holds together. Divide dough in half. Roll one half in an 8" circle and put on cookie sheet. Spread on jam, leaving 1" border. Roll remaining half in 8" circle and place on top. Press edges lightly to seal. Sprinkle with remaining sugar. Cut into 8 wedges, do not separate. Bake for 20 minutes. Makes 8 scones.

Cedar Rock Farm

3569 Mink Run Road • Frankfort, KY 40601
502-747-8754
Innkeepers: Rich and Lucy Clausen

Cedar Rock Farm offers a simple country getaway on a 110 acre sheep farm. Guests are invited to relax on the wraparound screened-in porch, curl up in a wingback chair with a good book, walk the forest trails, watch birds, stroll along the creek, or swim in the pool. The homegrown architecture of the farmhouse dates from the 1920's through an addition in 1993. Each of the three guest rooms is furnished with family antiques and has a private bath. Shelbyville and Frankfort sites and antique shops are a mere 20 minutes away. The charm and excitement of Louisville or Lexington are only a 45-minute drive.

Rates: $$ Includes full breakfast. Children over age 8 are welcome. No pets, please. Restricted smoking. We accept MasterCard and Visa.

Recipes From Cedar Rock Farm

BROWN BREAKFAST CASSEROLE

2 eggs, slightly beaten
1 cup yellow cornmeal
2 teaspoons baking soda
1 teaspoon salt (opt.)
17 ounce can cream-style corn
1 cup milk
1 pound lean sausage, browned & drained
1 large onion, chopped
1/4 - 1/2 cup chopped green pepper
2 cups shredded Cheddar cheese

Combine first six ingredients in bowl. Pour half the cornmeal mixture into greased 10 1/2" cast iron skillet. Sprinkle evenly with sausage, onions, and peppers. Top with cheese. Pour remaining cornmeal mixture evenly over the top. Bake at 350° for 45 to 50 minutes. Let stand 10 minutes before serving. Makes 6 - 8 servings.

WHOLE WHEAT BATTER BREAD

2 1/2 cups warm water
2 packages dry yeast
1/4 cup brown sugar
4 teaspoons salt
4 tablespoons soft shortening
2 cups whole wheat flour
4 cups white flour

Dissolve yeast in warm water; add brown sugar, salt, and shortening. Mix in wheat flour and white flour. Batter will be sticky. Cover and let rise until double. Stir down by beating 25 strokes, spread in 2 well-greased loaf pans, smooth out top with wet hand. Let rise until about double. Bake at 350° for 30 to 45 minutes. Makes 2 loaves.

Cliffview Resort

P.O. Box 65 • Rogers, KY 41365
606-668-6550
Innkeepers: Richard and Valerie White

1500 wooded acres include majestic cliffs, a natural arch, private lake and historic Lexington & Eastern Railroad bed. Enjoy fishing, wildlife, hiking, and horseback riding in breathtaking scenery. Nestled between two mountains lies our 15+ acre Clear Lake, excellent for fishing and canoeing. Investigate historic Lexington & Eastern Railroad track bed and discover for yourself 1,100' tunnel, the longest on the line, lying at the head of beautiful walker's creek. Plan a day hiking to Suzanna's Arch as you snap photos of majestic valleys, streams, cliffs, abundant wildlife. Trails for all ages, all levels. Two rooms available - private entrances, private baths, gorgeous view. **Cliffview Resort** is a truly unique experience and our excellent staff will do everything they can to enhance your visit. We treasure each guest and appreciate your comments and suggestions.

Rates: $$$ Includes full breakfast. No children or pets, please. Smoking is permitted. We accept MasterCard and Visa.

Recipes From Cliffview Resort

HAM & EGG PIE

1 cup shredded sharp Cheddar cheese
3 ounces sliced smoked ham, chopped, or 2/3 cup cooked ham, cut up
4 eggs, slightly beaten
2 tablespoons chopped green onion
2 cups milk
1/2 teaspoon salt
1/4 teaspoon dry mustard
1/8 teaspoon cayenne red pepper
2 cups unseasoned croutons

Spread cheese and ham in ungreased 9" pie plate. Mix remaining ingredients except croutons. Pour egg mixture over cheese and ham. Cover and refrigerate up to 24 hours. One hour and 15 minutes before serving, heat oven to 325°. Sprinkle egg mixture with croutons. Bake uncovered until knife inserted 1" from edge comes out clean, 50 to 55 minutes. Do not overbake. Let stand 10 minutes before serving. Makes 6 servings.

SAUSAGE QUICHES

11 ounce pkg. pie crust mix
1 pound sausage, browned & crumbled
6 tablespoons green onions, chopped
8 eggs, slightly beaten
4 cups whipping cream or light cream
1 1/2 teaspoons salt
1/2 teaspoon sugar
1/4 teaspoon cayenne red pepper

Prepare pastry for two one-crust pies as directed on pie crust mix. Brown sausage and onion, drain; and divide between pastry-lined pie plates. Beat eggs slightly, beat in whipping cream, salt, sugar, and red pepper. Heat oven to 425°. Pour half of the egg mixture on sausage and onions in each pie plate. Bake for 15 minutes. Reduce heat to 300° and bake until knife inserted 1" from edge comes out clean, about 45 minutes. Let stand 10 minutes before cutting. Makes 12 servings.

College Street Inn

223 South College Street • Franklin, KY 42134
502-586-9352   800-686-9352
Innkeepers: Mike and Donna Houston

Guests from across the U.S. and 26 countries have enjoyed Southern hospitality at this 100-year-old restored Queen Anne style Victorian home. Relax on the back porch, in the gazebo, or in one of our four uniquely decorated guest rooms. Enjoy antiques, queen size beds, private baths, and "Southern gourmet" breakfast. Easy access from I-65, 30 minutes from Bowling Green, 45 minutes from downtown Nashville.

Rates: $$ Includes full breakfast. No pets or smoking, please. We accept MasterCard and Visa.

BLUEBERRY CORN MUFFINS

2 1/4 cups flour
1 cup cornmeal
3/4 cup sugar
4 1/2 teaspoons baking powder
3 eggs
1 teaspoon vanilla
5 tablespoons butter, melted
1 1/2 cups buttermilk
1 cup fresh blueberries, or 1 cup frozen blueberries, drained

Combine dry ingredients in large bowl. Combine wet ingredients in small bowl. Stir wet into dry until just mixed. Gently fold in blueberries. Fill greased muffin cups 3/4 full. Bake at 375° for 25 minutes or until golden and firm. Makes 2 dozen muffins.

EGG PUFF

1/2 pound sliced mushrooms
1/2 cup melted butter
1/2 pound shredded Monterey Jack cheese
1 teaspoon baking powder
1/2 teaspoon salt
12 eggs
1/2 pound shredded Cheddar cheese
1/2 cup flour
1 pint cottage cheese

Preheat oven to 350°. Toss mushrooms in melted butter, just to coat. Beat eggs until light and fluffy. Add remaining ingredients. Stir in mushrooms and butter. Pour into greased 9" x 13" baking dish. Bake for 30 minutes. Makes 10 servings.

Ghent House Bed & Breakfast

411 Main Street, US 42, P.O. Box 478 • Ghent, KY 41045
606-291-0168 (weekdays)   502-347-5807 (anytime)
Innkeepers: Wayne G. and Diane J. Young

Built in 1833, **Ghent House** is an historic Federal style antebellum home with crystal chandeliers, fireplaces, private baths, jacuzzis, and private porches. English coachlights enhance the front entrance, a beautiful fantail window. Located halfway between Cincinnati and Louisville with a spectacular view of the Ohio River. Stroll through the rose garden with gazebo, walk the paths of the English walking garden. Enjoy the quiet and relaxation of yesteryear. "Come as a guest - Leave as a friend."

Rates: $$ - $$$ Includes full breakfast. Children are welcome. No pets, please. Restricted smoking. We accept MasterCard, Visa, and Am Ex.

Recipes From Ghent House Bed & Breakfast

AMISH CINNAMON RAISIN FRENCH TOAST

2 eggs
1/2 cup milk
1 teaspoon vanilla

Sliced cinnamon raisin bread
2 teaspoons cinnamon

Beat eggs, milk, and vanilla. Dip bread slices into mixture. Place in lightly greased skillet. Sprinkle with cinnamon, brown slightly, and turn bread. Sprinkle with more cinnamon, brown lightly. Serve with jam or jelly, powdered sugar, or syrup. Makes 6 - 8 servings.

BLUEBERRY KUCHEN

1 cup all-purpose flour
2 tablespoons sugar
Pinch of salt
1/2 cup butter or margarine, softened
1 tablespoon vinegar
1 cup sugar

2 tablespoons all-purpose flour
1/8 teaspoon ground cinnamon
3 cups fresh blueberries, divided
Powdered sugar

Combine first three ingredients; cut in butter with pastry blender until mixture resembles coarse meal. Sprinkle vinegar evenly over surface; stir with fork until all dry ingredients are moistened. Press pastry in bottom and 1" up sides of 9" springform pan. Combine 1 cup sugar, 2 tablespoons flour, and cinnamon, mixing well. Stir in 2 cups blueberries; spread evenly over pastry. Bake at 400° for 45 minutes. Remove from oven and sprinkle remaining 1 cup blueberries evenly over top. Chill well before removing from pan. Sprinkle with powdered sugar. Makes about 6 servings.

Glenmar Plantation Bed & Breakfast

2444 Valley Hill Road • Springfield, KY 40069
606-284-7791
Innkeeper: Ken Mandell

The Glenmar Plantation Bed & Breakfast is a lovely 250 acre horse farm located in Central Kentucky. The house was built in 1785 and boasts slave quarters and barns dating back to the 1700's. The home is furnished in antiques. **The Glenmar** has 8 guest rooms, one of which is our Kountry Kottage, a quaint little separate building. The grounds are home for many horses, cows, llamas, and other animals, that delight our guests.

Rates: $$$$ Includes full breakfast. Children are welcome. Pets are allowed. No smoking, please. We accept MasterCard, Visa, and Am Ex.

Recipes From Glenmar Plantation Bed & Breakfast

ADDICTION (POPPY SEED BREAD)

Glaze:
1/2 cup orange juice
1/2 teaspoon vanilla
3/4 cup sugar

Bread:
3 cups flour
1 1/2 teaspoons baking powder
3 eggs
1 1/2 cups low-fat milk
2 1/4 cups sugar
1 cup vegetable oil
1 1/2 teaspoons vanilla
1 teaspoon maple flavoring
1 1/2 tablespoons poppy seeds

For Glaze: Mix all ingredients for glaze together; set aside. Preheat oven to 350°. For Bread: Mix flour and baking powder in large bowl. In separate bowl mix together eggs, milk, sugar, oil, vanilla, and maple flavoring. Add to dry ingredients, mix well. Fold in poppy seeds. Put into 2 well-greased loaf pans and bake for one hour. Cool on cooling rack. Brush glaze on bread every 10 minutes until gone. Makes 2 loaves.

QUICHE

2 single pie crusts
6 eggs
2 cups sour cream
1 teaspoon Worcestershire sauce
1 teaspoon salt
2 cups coarsely shredded Swiss cheese
6 - 8 strips bacon, fried & crumbled
2 - 2.8 ounce cans French fried onions

Slightly beat eggs; add sour cream, Worcestershire sauce, and salt, and stir to mix. Add cheese, bacon, and onions. Pour evenly into pie crusts. Bake at 300° for 60 minutes. Makes 2 quiches.

Helton House Bed & Breakfast

103 East 23rd Street • Owensboro, KY 42303
502-926-7117
Innkeepers: Grace and Don Conley

We enjoy living in this 13 room, 4 bath home. Our wish is to make our guests enjoy the warmth, love, and relaxed atmosphere it offers. Each room is special to us. Our brick home was built in 1910 and features an Arts and Craft design with natural oak woodwork, hardwood floors with oriental rugs, and a second floor sun porch/television room. Each room is individually decorated with Laura Ashley or Ralph Lauren coverlets, wallpapers, etc. Antiques are scattered throughout. Owensboro is located in Western Kentucky on the Ohio River, and is 2 hours by car to either Nashville or Louisville. It features a new Riverpark Center for the Arts, and many antique stores and museums. In addition, the International Bluegrass Museum and the Bluegrass and Barbecue Festivals draw thousands of tourists each year.

Rates: $$ - $$$ Includes full breakfast. No children, pets, or smoking, please. We accept MasterCard and Visa.

BREAKFAST CASSEROLE

6 slices diet bread, crusts cut off, and buttered
1 pound sausage, cooked & crumbled
2 cups Cheddar cheese, shredded
6 eggs
2 cups half and half

Line casserole dish with buttered bread; spread cooked sausage over bread. Spread Cheddar cheese over sausage. Mix half and half with eggs and beat together. Pour over casserole. Cover. Refrigerate overnight. Take out 15 minutes before baking. Bake at 350° for 45 minutes.

STUFFED FRENCH TOAST

8 - 10 slices cubed white bread (French is good)
2 - 8 ounce pkgs. cream cheese, cut in very small cubes
2 cups milk
12 eggs, beaten
1 cup maple syrup

Place half of the cubed bread in 9" x 12" baking dish. Place cream cheese over top of bread. Add remaining bread on top. Beat together milk, eggs, and maple syrup. Pour over bread. Bake at 350° for 45 to 60 minutes, until brown.

Inn at the Park Bed & Breakfast

1332 South Fourth Street • Louisville, KY 40208
502-637-6930
Innkeepers: John and Sandra Mullins

Inn at the Park was built in 1886 by Russell Houston, a co-founder and attorney for the L&N Railroad. The 7,400 square-foot mansion was restored to its former elegance in 1985 and has once again claimed its place as a "Queen" of Old Louisville. Adjacent to Central Park in historic Old Louisville, which boasts the largest collection of Victorian homes in America, it is one of the finest examples of Richardsonian Romanesque architecture remaining in the United States. A sweeping, grand staircase, rich hardwood floors, fireplaces and balconies, views of the park, and elegant period furnishings will whisk you back to a bygone era while modern amenities and full, gourmet breakfasts will make your stay a truly pleasant and memorable one.

Rates: $$ - $$$$ Includes full breakfast. No children or pets, please. Restricted smoking. We accept MasterCard, Visa, and Am Ex.

Recipes From Inn at the Park Bed & Breakfast

ITALIAN SAUSAGE FRITTATA

1/2 cup steamed Yukon Gold yellow potatoes, sliced or cubed
2 tablespoons Italian sausage, previously fried & crumbled
2 eggs
1 tablespoon water
1 tablespoon mixed fresh herbs, chopped*
Salt and pepper, to taste
Cheddar cheese, shredded
Roma tomato slices & green onion for garnish

Butter 7" skillet and briefly sauté potatoes. Add sausage and briefly sauté. Beat eggs with water, herbs, *(fresh oregano, chives, thyme, basil, etc.) salt, and pepper and pour over potato-sausage mixture. Cover and cook until almost set. Place skillet under preheated broiler and broil until eggs are completely set on top. Remove from broiler and sprinkle with Cheddar cheese. Arrange 3 tomato slices on top in decorative pattern, sprinkle with chopped green onion, and broil briefly, just until cheese melts. Makes 1 serving.

STUFFED FRENCH TOAST

4 slices Pepperidge Farm Vienna bread
Cream cheese, softened
Seedless blackberry preserves
Chopped pecans
Melted butter for sautéing
Powdered sugar

Custard:
2 eggs
1/2 cup half and half
1 tablespoon sugar
1/2 teaspoon cinnamon
1 tablespoon Grand Marnier
Freshly ground nutmeg

Spread one side of one slice of bread thinly with softened cream cheese. Spread another slice with a thin layer of preserves. Sprinkle chopped pecans on cream cheese slice and place bread slices together with ingredients inside, forming a sandwich. Mix custard ingredients in shallow dish and dip sandwich in custard, coating it on both sides. Place melted butter in hot sauté pan and sauté the French toast until nicely browned on each side. Sprinkle with powdered sugar and serve warm with maple syrup and fresh fruit. Makes 2 servings.

L & N Bed & Breakfast

327 North Main Street • Henderson, KY 42420
502-831-1100
Innkeepers: Norris and Mary Elizabeth Priest

L & N is a two-story Victorian home featuring oaken floors, woodwork, stained glass, antique furnishings, and a convenient location in the heart of downtown Henderson, next door to RR overpass. Four bedrooms are available, each with private bath, direct dial telephone and cable TV in each bedroom. John James Audubon Park & Museum is only 3 1/2 miles away and open year-round. Your innkeepers reside next door.

Rates: $$ Includes continental plus breakfast. Children are welcome. No pets or smoking, please.

Recipes From L & N Bed & Breakfast

BREAKFAST QUICHE

6 slices white bread, cubed
1 pound sausage, cooked & drained
6 eggs
1 teaspoon dry mustard
2 cups milk
1 cup shredded Cheddar cheese

Place bread in bottom of 9" x 13" baking dish. Fry sausage, drain grease; layer meat on top of bread. Beat eggs; add dry mustard, milk, and cheese. Pour over bread in dish. Can be refrigerated overnight. Bake at 350° for 30 minutes or until done. Makes 8 servings.

HAM & CHEESE SQUARES

2 cups Bisquick mix
3/4 cup chopped ham
1 cup shredded Cheddar cheese
1/2 cup grated Parmesan cheese
1/4 cup sour cream
1 tablespoon parsley flakes
1/2 teaspoon salt
2/3 cup milk
1 egg

Preheat oven to 350°. Grease 9" x 13" x 2" pan. Mix all ingredients together and spread in pan. Bake until golden brown, 25 to 30 minutes. Cut in squares and serve with fruit. Makes 6 - 8 servings.

Lafayette Heights Clubhouse

173 Lafayette Heights • Marion, KY 41064
502-965-3889
Innkeepers: Harley and Joyce Haegelin

The original clubhouse was built in the early 1920's, a focal point of social activity for the employees of Lafayette Fluorspar Company. It was converted into a rest home for the elderly after being sold by U.S. Steel. Purchased by the current owners as a retirement project; it has become a twenty year "somewhat ongoing" remodeling effort. All the interior decorating was planned and executed by Joyce with Harley supplying the "hammer and saw" muscle. All electrical, plumbing, and fire safety systems have been upgraded by professionals. The clubhouse offers seven bedrooms - six with private baths. The honeymoon suite includes a jacuzzi. Centrally located to many of Western Kentucky's major attractions.

Rates: $ Includes full, continental plus, or continental breakfast. Children are welcome. No pets or smoking, please. We accept MasterCard and Visa.

Recipes From Lafayette Heights Clubhouse

EGG BLOSSOMS

Egg cups:
- 4 sheets phyllo pastry
- 2 tablespoons butter, melted
- 4 teaspoons grated Parmesan cheese
- 4 eggs
- 4 teaspoons minced green onions
- Salt and freshly ground pepper, to taste

Tomato Sauce:
- 16 ounce can whole tomatoes, undrained, chopped
- 1 clove garlic, minced
- 1/2 cup chopped onion
- 1 tablespoon white wine vinegar
- 1/4 teaspoon dried leaf oregano
- 1/2 teaspoon salt

For egg cups: Preheat oven to 350°. Grease 4 - 2 1/2" muffin cups. Brush 1 sheet of phyllo with butter. Top with another sheet; brush with butter. Cut stack into 6 - 4" squares. Repeat with remaining 2 sheets. Stack 3 squares together, rotating so corners do not overlap. Press into greased muffin cup. Repeat with remaining squares. Sprinkle 1 teaspoon cheese into each phyllo-lined cup. Break 1 egg into each cup. Sprinkle onion over eggs. Season with salt & pepper. Bake 15 to 20 minutes or until pastry is golden & eggs are set. Serve with tomato sauce. For tomato sauce: Combine all ingredients in medium saucepan. Cook, stirring occasionally, over medium heat until onion is tender, about 20 minutes. Makes 4 servings.

MUSHROOM & ONION EGG BAKE

- 1 tablespoon vegetable oil
- 4 green onions, chopped
- 4 ounces mushrooms, sliced
- 1 cup low-fat cottage cheese
- 1 cup sour cream
- 6 eggs
- 2 tablespoons all-purpose flour
- 1/4 teaspoon salt
- 1/8 teaspoon freshly ground pepper
- Dash of hot pepper sauce

Preheat oven to 350°. Grease shallow 1-quart baking dish. Heat oil in medium skillet over medium heat. Add onions and mushrooms; cook until tender. Set aside. In blender or food processor, process cottage cheese until almost smooth. Add remaining ingredients, process until combined. Stir in onions and mushrooms, pour into greased dish. Bake about 40 minutes or until knife inserted near center comes out clean. Makes 6 servings.

Licking Riverside Historic Bed & Breakfast

516 Garrard Street • Covington, KY 41011
606-291-0191   800-GUESTBB
Innkeeper: Lynda L. Freeman

Located in the Historic District - on the Licking River! Jacuzzi Suite has 2 rooms with a jacuzzi room, jacuzzi for two on platform with river view. Bedroom has sitting area, TV, VCR, refrigerator, fireplace, and air-conditioning with European decor. Three story hairpin staircase. Beautiful decor, Victorian European in flavor. Also deluxe Queen room with wrought iron bed - private bath, TV, and VCR. Airport pick-up. Small wedding, business, and professional guests welcome.

Rates: $$$ - $$$$ Includes continental plus breakfast. No pets, please. Restricted smoking. We accept MasterCard, Visa, and Am Ex.

Recipes From Licking Riverside Historic B & B

BASIC FOUNDATION DOUGH

2 cakes compressed yeast
1 tablespoon sugar
1 cup warm (not hot) water
1 cup milk, scalded
3/4 cup shortening
1/2 cup sugar
1 teaspoon salt
7 cups sifted all-purpose flour
3 eggs, beaten

Dissolve yeast and 1 tablespoon sugar in lukewarm water. Add shortening, 1/2 cup sugar, and salt to scalded milk and cool to lukewarm. Add 3 cups flour to make a batter, and beat with wooden spoon. Add yeast mixture and beaten eggs; beat well. Add enough of remaining flour to make soft dough, turn out on floured surface and knead lightly. Place in greased bowl, turn so that all sides are greased and let rise until doubled in bulk, about 2 hours. When light, punch dough down and shape as desired for Coffee Cake, Swedish Tea Ring or Cinnamon Buns. When ready to bake, bake in preheated oven at 425° for 12 to 25 minutes, depending on size. *We use this recipe to make numerous items. Especially good are the Cinnamon Buns. Guests love them! They are delicious with or without icing. Serve warm to melt their hearts and stomachs.

Maple Hill Manor Bed & Breakfast

2941 Perryville Road • Springfield, KY 40069
606-336-3075   800-886-7546
Innkeepers: Bob and Kay Carroll

Stately hilltop manor, circa 1851 brick Revival, on National Register of Historic Places. It features a 13 1/2' ceiling, and a cherry spiral staircase. Seven guest rooms beautifully furnished with antiques, all with private baths. Some rooms with canopy beds, jacuzzi, or gas fireplace. Homemade dessert served in evenings in front of fireplace.

Rates: $$ - $$$ Includes full breakfast. Children are welcome. No pets or smoking, please. We accept MasterCard and Visa.

Recipes From Maple Hill Manor Bed & Breakfast

BREAKFAST DELIGHT

2 cans creamy onion soup
3 ounces cream cheese
32 ounce bag frozen hash brown potatoes
1/2 cup shredded Cheddar cheese
1/3 cup shredded mozzarella cheese

Grease 9" x 13" pan. Mix all ingredients together in large mixing bowl. Pour mixture into pan. Bake at 400° for 40 minutes. Sprinkle mozzarella cheese on top after baking. Makes 10 - 14 servings.

EGGS GOLDENROD

4 hard-cooked eggs
2 tablespoons margarine
2 tablespoons all-purpose flour
1 cup milk
1/2 teaspoon salt
6 slices bread, no crust
3 tablespoons melted margarine
Paprika for garnish

Slice one egg in half, remove yolk and mince it, set aside. Chop egg white and remaining eggs, set aside. Melt 2 tablespoons margarine in heavy pan over low heat. Add flour, stir until smooth. Add milk a little at a time, cook over medium heat until thickened and bubbly. Stir in salt and chopped eggs. Trim crust from bread. Brush both sides of bread with melted margarine. Press each slice into the cup of a muffin tin. Bake at 400° for 8 to 10 minutes. Remove cups and place on serving plate. Spoon egg mixture into cups. Garnish with minced yolk and paprika. Makes 6 servings.

GRITS PATTIES

1/3 cup uncooked regular grits
2 tablespoons self-rising flour
1/4 teaspoon salt
1/8 teaspoon pepper
1 egg, slightly beaten
Hot vegetable oil for frying

Cook grits according to package directions. Stir in flour, salt, pepper, and egg. Mix well. Drop mixture by tablespoonfuls into hot oil. Gently flatten with spatula. Brown on both sides; drain on paper towels. Serve immediately. Makes 8 servings.

HERB BREAD

3 cups all-purpose flour
2 tablespoons sugar
1 tablespoon baking powder
2 teaspoons caraway seed
1/2 teaspoon salt
1/2 teaspoon dried whole thyme
1/2 teaspoon ground nutmeg
1 egg, beaten
1 1/2 cups milk
1/2 cup vegetable oil

Combine flour, sugar, baking powder, and seasonings into large bowl. Stir well. Combine remaining ingredients; add to dry ingredients, stirring just until moistened. Spoon into greased 8 1/2" x 4 1/2" x 3" pan. Bake at 350° for 50 to 55 minutes or until a wooden pick comes out clean. Makes 1 loaf.

Recipes From Maple Hill Manor Bed & Breakfast

MAPLE HILL SPECIAL

1/4 cup melted margarine
1/4 cup flour
4 eggs, beaten
2 cups shredded Monterey Jack cheese
1 cup cottage cheese
1 1/2 ounces green chilies, chopped
Green pepper slices, small tomato slices & Parmesan cheese for garnish

Mix first two ingredients, then add eggs. Add shredded cheese and cottage cheese, then chilies. Pour into greased 11" x 7" glass baking dish. Bake at 350° for 30 minutes. Cut into six pieces and put a small slice of green pepper and tomato on top of each piece. Top with Parmesan cheese to taste. Makes 6 servings.

SPRINGFIELD COFFEE CAKE

1 box yellow cake mix
4 eggs
1/2 cup oil
12 ounces sour cream
1 small box instant vanilla pudding
1/4 cup sugar
1 1/2 teaspoons cinnamon

Mix all ingredients together except sugar and cinnamon. Pour half of mixture into greased bundt pan. Mix together sugar and cinnamon. Sprinkle over batter and then cut through with a knife to swirl. Add remainder of batter. Bake at 325° for one hour. Cool for 25 minutes, then remove from pan.

The Marcum-Porter House Bed & Breakfast

P.O. Box 369 • Stearns, KY 42647
606-376-2242
Innkeepers: Pat Porter Newton and Charles and Sandra Porter

Located in the heart of the Big South Fork National Recreation Area, a charming home (1904) offers gracious accommodations for guests with interests in history and scenic beauty. Air-conditioning. Gourmet breakfasts served in formal dining room. Spacious grounds. Nearby attractions include Scenic Railway, 9-hole golf course, museum, hiking, horseback riding, whitewater rafting and fishing, and beautiful Cumberland Falls.

Rates: $$ Includes full breakfast. Children over age 6 are welcome. No pets, please. Restricted smoking. We accept personal checks and MasterCard and Visa.

Recipes From The Marcum-Porter House B & B

BETTY SMITH'S HAM BISCUITS

2 cups self-rising flour
1/4 cup Crisco
2/3 cup milk

Butter for biscuits
Cooked country ham slices, very thin

Mix flour and Crisco. Add milk. Roll dough out and cut out small biscuits, not too thick. Bake at 450° for 8 minutes. Remove from oven. Split each biscuit and butter it. Place ham slice in each biscuit. Freeze. To serve, bake again at 450° for 8 minutes. Biscuits may be frozen or thawed before second baking.

OATMEAL WAFFLES

1 1/2 cups all-purpose flour
1 cup quick-cooking rolled oats
1 tablespoon baking powder
1/2 teaspoon cinnamon

1/4 teaspoon salt
2 eggs, beaten
1 1/2 cups milk
6 tablespoons butter, melted
2 tablespoons brown sugar

In large mixing bowl, stir together flour, oats, baking powder, cinnamon, and salt; set aside. In small mixing bowl stir together eggs, milk, melted butter, and brown sugar. Add to flour mixture; stir until blended. Pour batter onto grids of preheated, lightly greased waffle iron. *A hearty waffle that "sticks to your ribs" better than a regular waffle!

Myers' Bed & Breakfast

124 East Depot Street • Marion, KY 42064
502-965-3731
Innkeepers: J. D. and Merle Myers (Jim)

Myers' Bed & Breakfast, an 1880's Victorian home was completely renovated before opening as a B&B in 1994. The large front porch welcomes guests to enjoy the wicker swing before entering the parlor with its intricate gingerbread archway and the pocket doors leading to the library. The original moldings and hardwood floors are throughout the house. The three bedrooms upstairs are named after grandchildren. Scarlett and J. D.'s room share a bath, Victoria's room has a private bath. Scarlett and Victoria's rooms have 4-poster queen size beds. J. D.'s has twin beds. The cottage has 2 rooms with queen beds and private baths. One room has loft and is handicapped accessible. Guests may enjoy a full breakfast in either the dining room or on back porch.

Rates: $ - $$ Includes full breakfast. Children are welcome. No pets, please. Restricted smoking.

Recipes From Myers' Bed & Breakfast

POTATO CHIP COOKIES

1 pound margarine
1 cup sugar
1 teaspoon vanilla

3 1/2 cups flour, sifted
1 1/2 cups crushed potato chips

Cream together margarine and sugar. Add remaining ingredients and mix well. Drop by teaspoonfuls onto ungreased cookie sheet - 1/2" apart. Bake at 350° for 12 to 15 minutes. While cookies are warm, roll in powdered sugar. Makes about 100 small cookies.

PUMPKIN PANCAKES

2 cups Bisquick mix
2 tablespoons light brown sugar
2 teaspoons cinnamon
1 teaspoon allspice
1/2 cup pumpkin

1 1/2 cups (12 oz.) evaporated milk
2 tablespoons oil
2 eggs
1 teaspoon vanilla

In bowl mix Bisquick, brown sugar, cinnamon, and allspice. Add pumpkin, milk, oil, eggs, and vanilla. Beat with mixer until smooth. Pour 1/4 - 1/3 cup batter onto heated and lightly greased griddle. Cook until golden, then turn and cook other side. Makes 16 pancakes.

Myrtledene Bed & Breakfast

370 North Spalding Avenue • Lebanon, KY 40033
800-391-1721
Innkeeper: James Spragens

Built in 1833, **Myrtledene** was the headquarters of General John Hunt Morgan during his Lebanon raids of the Civil War. Furnished throughout in antiques. Enjoy breakfast in the dining room, on the patio, in the garden, on the balcony, or in your room. An opulent home perfect for a romantic getaway, family vacation, or lodging during business travel. Attractions include Makers Mark Distillery, Lincoln Homestead, Historic Bardstown, Gethsemane Abbey, Penn's Store (America's oldest general store), and Loretto Motherhouse. Four guest rooms. Banquet/reception/conference facility.

Rates: $$ Includes full breakfast. Children are welcome. No pets, please. Restricted smoking. We accept MasterCard and Visa.

Recipes From Myrtledene Bed & Breakfast

MYRTLEDENE ARTICHOKE OMELET

3 eggs
3 tablespoons milk or half and half
Salt and freshly ground pepper, to taste

4 tablespoons butter
3 sliced artichoke hearts
Freshly grated Parmesan cheese, to taste

Beat eggs, milk, salt, and pepper well. Add 2 tablespoons butter to omelet pan over low to medium heat. Add egg mixture. When eggs cook on bottom, press in sides with spatula to allow liquid to run down to the bottom of the pan to cook. When nearly all of omelet has cooked, top with artichokes which have been lightly sautéed in 2 tablespoons butter. Add Parmesan cheese to cover omelet. Remove from pan onto plate by sliding out half and folding over with other half. *Do not allow eggs to cook fast. Makes 1 serving.

STRAWBERRY CHEESECAKE FRENCH TOAST

1 cup ricotta cheese
3 tablespoons powdered sugar
1 tablespoon vanilla extract
16 - 1/3" slices French or Italian bread

2 large eggs
1 cup milk
1 1/2 tablespoons butter
2 cups sliced strawberries
Strawberry syrup
Powdered sugar for garnish

Stir together ricotta cheese, powdered sugar, and vanilla until smooth. Spread 8 bread slices with mixture, top with remaining bread, like a sandwich. In bowl beat eggs and milk. Add butter to frying pan over medium heat. Dip bread in egg mixture to saturate. Fry on each side until golden brown - about 5 minutes for each side. Place strawberry slices on top. Pour syrup over sandwich and dust with powdered sugar. Makes 4 - 8 servings.

Old Louisville Inn Bed & Breakfast

1359 South Third Street • Louisville, KY 40208
502-635-1574
Innkeeper: Marianne Lesher

Located in historic Old Louisville, 10 minutes from airport, downtown, and Churchill Downs. Wake up to the aroma of freshly baked muffins or popovers - when you stay in one of our guest rooms or suites. We offer eleven guest rooms. Enjoy a stroll through St. James Court, tour historic homes, go antique shopping, or just relax with a cup of tea; you will feel right at home.

Rates: $$$ Includes full breakfast. Children are welcome. No pets, please. Restricted smoking. We accept MasterCard and Visa.

Recipes From Old Louisville Inn Bed & Breakfast

BANANA BREAD

1/2 pound melted butter	1 teaspoon baking soda
2 cups sugar	1 teaspoon baking powder
5 ripe bananas, mashed	1 teaspoon salt
4 eggs	1 1/2 teaspoons nutmeg
2 3/4 cups all-purpose flour	

Optional topping:

1/2 cup flour	4 tablespoons cold butter
1/2 cup sugar	1 cup chopped pecans (opt.)
Cinnamon, to taste	

use PAM

~~Grease 3 loaf pans.~~ Cream butter and sugar together; add bananas and eggs, one at a time. Mix dry ingredients together. Add to banana mixture until blended. Pour batter into prepared baking tins. For topping: Mix flour, sugar, and cinnamon. Cut in cold butter until crumbly. Add pecans if desired. Bake at 350° for one hour. Makes 3 medium loaves.

POP-OVERS

4 extra large eggs	1 cup all-purpose flour
1 cup milk	1 teaspoon salt
1/3 cup melted butter	

Blend ingredients in order with an old-fashioned egg beater in a 4-cup measuring bowl. Spray pop-over tin heavily with vegetable spray. Pour batter in tin. Bake at 400° for 45 minutes. Temperature and time may vary with altitude and ovens. Remove from oven when golden. Poke holes in tops to let out steam. Serve hot with butter, honey, and jams. *Mini-Version: Spray mini-muffin tin, pour 24. Prepare batter and bake as above. After cooking, may be stuffed with homemade chicken, crab, or tuna salad, or use a pastry tube to pipe in chocolate or strawberry mousse. Enjoy for a light lunch.

Old Talbott Tavern/McLean House

107 West Stephen Foster Avenue • Bardstown, KY 40004
502-348-3494   800-4TAVERN
Innkeepers: The Kelley Family

The historic **Talbott Tavern** was built in 1779; we remain the oldest western stagecoach stop in America. We were licensed by Patrick Henry. Stay in our guest rooms that Abraham Lincoln, General Patton, Jesse James, and other notable persons have slept in. Six rooms have private baths, TV's, and beautiful antiques. **The McLean House** was built in 1814. This beautiful building housed Bardstown's first post office where pegs for "Wanted" posters still remain. It served as a hospital during the Civil War. Seven rooms (5 have private baths) have wonderful antiques and TV's.

Rates: $ - $$$ Includes continental breakfast. Children are welcome. No pets, please. Smoking is permitted. We accept MasterCard and Visa.

Recipes From Old Talbott Tavern/McLean House

GARLIC GRITS

2 1/4 cups water
1/2 teaspoon salt
1/2 cup grits
1/2 stick margarine
1 roll garlic cheese
1 egg

1 cup crushed Corn
 Flakes cereal
Milk as needed
Extra margarine as
 needed
Dash of paprika

Add salt to water and boil. Add grits slowly and cook 3 to 5 minutes, stirring occasionally. Take off heat, add margarine, and garlic cheese. Stir until melted. Beat egg in measuring cup and finish filling with milk to make 1/2 cup. Add to grits mixture. Pour into well-greased baking dish. Sprinkle with crushed Corn Flakes. Dot with margarine and dash of paprika. Bake uncovered in pan of water at 350° for one hour. Makes 6 - 8 servings.

OLD TALBOTT TAVERN CORN FRITTERS

2 cups self-rising flour
1/4 teaspoon sugar
1 egg

1/4 cup whole kernel corn
Milk as needed
Powdered sugar

Mix flour, sugar, egg, and corn, adding just enough milk to moisten. Batter should be stiff. Drop by tablespoons into deep oil at 325° and fry to a golden brown. Drain, roll in powdered sugar, and serve warm.

The Oldham House Bed & Breakfast and Antiques

111 South Main Street, P.O. Box 628 • New Castle, KY 40050
502-845-0103
Innkeeper: Emmy Houweling

A Federal period structure built in 1820, **The Oldham House** is located a short distance from the Bluegrass Region and convenient to Louisville, Lexington, and Cincinnati. The B&B is decorated in country antiques and accessories, most of which are for sale at Emmy's Antiques Shop located on the property. The kitchen had once been the slave kitchen with separate quarters above. The original smokehouse still remains on the tree-filled, park-like property. Things to do include horse racing, visiting scenic Ohio River towns, fishing state parks, golfing, and of course, antiquing, and just relaxing on the deck or patio.

Rates: $$ Includes full breakfast. Children over age 12 are welcome. No pets or smoking, please.

Recipes From The Oldham House B &B and Antiques

CINNAMON CROISSANTS

1 tube refrigerator crescent rolls
Cinnamon, to taste
Sugar, to taste
Crushed walnuts

Unroll crescent dough according to directions on tube. Mix together cinnamon, sugar, and nuts. Sprinkle on the inside of dough; roll up according to directions. Sprinkle more cinnamon-sugar mixture on top. Bake according to directions. *Variation: May be baked with chocolate chips inside, instead of cinnamon-sugar. Makes 6 servings.

EGG MEDLEY

8 eggs (2 per serving)
2 tablespoons milk
4 slices crumbled bacon
1 teaspoon chopped green spring onion
1/4 cup chopped green peppers
1/4 cup frozen or fresh corn
Salt & pepper, to taste
1/2 cup grated cheese
4 thin slices of tomato
1/4 cup toasted wheat germ

Beat eggs and milk together. Cook and crumble bacon, add to eggs. Set aside. Sauté onion, green peppers, and corn in a little margarine in large Teflon skillet until just barely soft. Pour eggs over sautéed mixture; add salt and pepper. Sprinkle with grated cheese, arrange tomato slices on top. Cook slowly with lid on, until set. Sprinkle with toasted wheat germ. Cut into 4 wedges, and serve with fresh fruit for garnish. Serve with toasted flying saucers, (medium pocket bread sliced lengthwise, available at grocer's deli) or English muffins. Makes 4 servings.

Osbornes of Cabin Hollow

111 Fietz Orchard Road • Somerset, KY 42501
606-382-5495
Innkeepers: Robert and Mary Osborne

Tucked away, 4 miles from Somerset, in the hills, among the trees and rocks, looking down on the lights of the city, you will find our dream home built of logs. We invite you to come and share the peace and tranquility of this place with us. Swing on the porch, walk in the woods, or just relax. Enjoy a light or hearty country breakfast (including scratch biscuits) in our spacious windowed great room, where the view is terrific! Our jellies and preserves are some of Kentucky's finest and are available for purchase. We offer one guest suite with private bath, entrance, and deck. Two rooms with shared bath. Cabin Hollow is easy access to Lake Cumberland, Big South Fork, Cumberland Falls, Daniel Boone National Forest, and Renfro Valley. Hospitality at it's best!

Rates: $$ Includes full breakfast. Children over age 12 are welcome. No pets, please. Restricted smoking. We accept MasterCard and Visa.

Recipes From Osbornes of Cabin Hollow

MARY'S SCRATCH BISCUITS

2 cups self-rising White Lily flour
1/4 cup Crisco
3/4 cup milk
1/4 teaspoon baking powder

Put flour into bowl, make hole in center. Add shortening and baking powder. Cut in shortening. Add milk. Mix well until dough leaves sides of bowl clean. Turn out onto lightly floured surface and knead gently about 10 times. Roll dough about 1/2" thick and cut out. Place on greased cookie sheet and bake at 400° for 12 minutes or until golden brown. Makes 1 dozen biscuits.

HEAVENLY SCENT COFFEE CAKE

1/2 cup chopped pecans
1 pkg. Rich's frozen dough balls
1 box regular butterscotch pudding mix
1 stick margarine
1/4 cup brown sugar
Pinch of cinnamon

Spray bottom and sides of bundt pan with cooking spray. Cover with pecans. Place frozen dough balls on top of nuts, sprinkle with dry pudding mix. Melt butter or margarine and mix with brown sugar. Sprinkle over top of dough. Sprinkle with cinnamon. Cover with damp tea towel and let rise overnight. Bake at 350° for 25 to 30 minutes or until brown and will leave sides of pan. Turn upside down on pretty plate and serve warm. Makes 6 - 8 servings.

Pineapple Inn Bed & Breakfast

645 South Broadway • Georgetown, KY 40324
502-868-5453
Innkeepers: Les Olsen and Muriel Konietzko

VICTORIAN SUITE - Step back in time to a room full of Victorian touches. Full size bed, private Victorian bath with claw foot tub, lots of light and privacy, with separate entrance. COUNTRY SUITE - Make yourself cozy in this special room with full private bath and full size bed with country quilts and accessories. Lots of extra touches to give a most pleasurable night's sleep away in the country. AMERICANA ROOM - All things American, from the iron beds to the flags on the wall. Loaded with top quality antiques. This room is able to accommodate families comfortably; sleeps up to six. Detached private bath. DERBY ROOM - The most luxurious of all the suites. Includes full bath with hot tub/spa. Beautifully decorated in a gentleman's print wallpaper with Equestrian motif. Queen size canopy bed with large sitting area. As always, a full gourmet breakfast is served each morning. Reservations required.

Rates: $$ - $$$ Includes full breakfast. Children are welcome. No pets, please. Restricted smoking. We accept MasterCard and Visa.

Recipes From Pineapple Inn Bed & Breakfast

CORNUCOPIA'S CROISSANTS À L'ORANGE

6 croissants
9 ounce jar orange marmalade
3 ounces orange juice
5 eggs
1 cup heavy cream
1 teaspoon almond extract
Strawberries and mandarin orange sections, for garnish

Cut croissants in half lengthwise and place bottom halves in buttered 9" x 12" ovenproof dish. Thin marmalade with orange juice and spoon over each half, saving a little for glaze. Replace croissant tops. Beat eggs, cream, and almond extract. Pour over top of croissants. Spoon some thinned marmalade over top. Soak overnight in refrigerator. Remove 45 minutes before baking. Bake in preheated 350° oven for about 25 minutes. Serve hot and garnish with strawberries and mandarin orange sections. Makes 6 servings.

SWEDISH EGG COFFEE

7 cups water
1 egg
2 tablespoons water
1/3 cup regular grind coffee
1/2 cup cold water

Bring 7 cups water to boil in heavy enameled coffee pot. Meanwhile, in small bowl beat egg and 2 tablespoons water; stir in coffee. When water boils, add coffee-egg mixture. Boil gently for 7 minutes. Remove from heat; add 1/2 cup cold water. Grounds will settle to the bottom. Makes 10 servings.

Randolph House

463 West Lexington • Danville, KY 40422
606-236-9594
Innkeeper: Georgie Heizer

Southern hospitality enhances a visit to **Randolph House**, an antebellum home located near downtown Danville and Centre College Campus. Furnished with family heirlooms and European antiques, the parlor and library invite guests to find a book or enjoy a conversation. Three bedrooms with queen bed, bath en suite, television, and telephone ensure a comfortable sojourn. An additional twin bed can accommodate an additional person in two rooms. Upstairs a coffee pot and refrigerator provide beverages. Breakfasts served with Victorian appointments are a memorable way to begin a day.

Rates: $$ Includes full breakfast. Children are welcome. Pets are allowed with prior permission only. Restricted smoking. We accept MasterCard, Visa, and Am Ex.

Recipes From Randolph House

KENTUCKY COFFEE CAKE

Cake:
1 1/2 cups brown sugar
4 eggs
1 cup applesauce
1/2 cup orange juice
2 1/2 teaspoons vanilla extract
3 cups flour
3 teaspoons baking powder

Filling:
1/3 cup white sugar
1/4 cup brown sugar
1/2 cup flour
2 teaspoons cinnamon
2 tablespoons cold butter, cut into small pieces
1/2 cup chopped nuts

Cream together brown sugar and eggs. Add applesauce, orange juice, and vanilla extract. Add flour and baking powder. Mix together filling ingredients. Heat oven to 350°. Grease and flour large tube pan. Put in half of the batter. Cover with 3/4 filling mixture. Pour remainder of batter onto filling. Sprinkle with remaining filling. Bake 1 1/2 hours or until toothpick inserted comes out clean. *Can be baked the night before and reheated in foil in the morning.) Makes 12 servings.

RANDOLPH HOUSE FRITTATA

1/2 pound Cheddar cheese, grated
1/2 pound Swiss cheese, grated
6 eggs, separated
1/3 cup bread crumbs
1 can evaporated milk
1/2 cup picante sauce

Preheat oven to 375°. Grease 10" pie pan, and spread cheeses across bottom of pan. Beat egg yolks, add bread crumbs, and milk. Beat egg whites, and fold into bread crumb mixture. Pour into prepared pan. Top with picante sauce. Bake for 45 minutes. Makes 6 - 8 servings.

The RidgeRunner Bed & Breakfast

208 Arthur Heights • Middlesboro, KY 40965
606-248-4299
Innkeepers: Sue Richards and Irma Gall

The RidgeRunner B&B is a restored 1890 Victorian home, that sits on a ridge overlooking downtown Middlesboro, and has a vista of the Cumberland Mountain range. The large 60' porch welcomes guests with vintage rocking chairs, porch swings, iced tea, or lemonade, a challenging game of croquet, or the relaxation of birds singing, or leaves rustling to the mountain breezes. Two guest rooms have private baths, while two guest rooms share a bath. All rooms are comfortably furnished with period antiques, and family heirlooms. The hosts have unique stories to share with their guests, of life in Appalachia from the 1950's. Ask about their experiences, very delightful.

Rates: $$ Includes continental plus breakfast. Children over age 12 are welcome. No pets, please. Restricted smoking.

BLACK ROCK BAKED OATMEAL

1/3 cup oil
1/2 cup sugar
1 large egg, beaten
2 cups quick-cooking oats (oatmeal)
1 1/2 teaspoons baking powder
1/2 teaspoon salt
3/4 cup milk

Mix together oil, sugar, and egg. In separate bowl, mix together remaining ingredients. Mix wet and dry ingredients together. Pour into greased 8" x 8" pan. Bake at 350° for 25 to 30 minutes. You can add raisins or other dried fruit, before baking, or garnish with spiced apple rings. *This recipe can be doubled, and poured into greased 9" x 13" pan. Makes 6 servings.

STUFFED APRICOT FRENCH TOAST

8 ounces cream cheese
1 1/2 teaspoons vanilla (divided)
1/2 cup finely chopped walnuts
1 loaf French bread, cut into 1 1/2" slices
4 eggs
1 cup heavy cream
1/2 teaspoon ground nutmeg
1 jar apricot preserves
1/2 cup orange juice

Beat cream cheese and 1 teaspoon vanilla until fluffy. Add nuts. Cut French bread into 1 1/2" slices, cut a pocket in the top of each slice. Fill each pocket with 2 tablespoons of cream cheese mixture. In another bowl, beat eggs, cream, nutmeg and 1/2 teaspoon vanilla. Dip both sides of bread into egg mixture, being careful not to squeeze cream mixture. Cook on lightly greased griddle until golden brown. Place on ungreased baking sheet, bake at 300° for 20 minutes. Combine preserves and orange juice - drizzle over toast. Makes 8 servings.

Rocking Horse Manor Bed & Breakfast

1022 South Third Street • Louisville, KY 40203
502-583-0408   888-HORSEBB
Innkeeper: Diana Jachimiak

A Richardsonian Romanesque mansion built in 1888, the **Rocking Horse Manor B&B** combines old world charm with modern amenities in each of its five guest rooms. All rooms have cable television, telephone, central air/heat control, and private in-room bath. Conveniently located near Churchill Downs, downtown Louisville, Commonwealth Convention Center, Louisville International Airport, Kentucky Center for the Arts, J. B. Speed Art Museum, University of Louisville & Spalding University, Kentucky Fair & Exposition Center and antique shops. Relax at the end of your day in our large Victorian parlor or library with wet bar, or choose our third-floor sitting area with a mini-office. Full gourmet breakfast offers muffins, quiches, breads, and fresh fruits. Complimentary evening snacks and beverages also available.

Rates: $$ - $$$$ Includes full breakfast. Children are welcome. No pets, please. Restricted smoking. We accept MasterCard, Visa, and Am Ex.

Recipes From Rocking Horse Manor B & B

BLUEBERRY BREAKFAST PUDDING

4 cups drained fruit (blueberries or peaches)	1 teaspoon baking powder
1/2 cup sugar	1 teaspoon salt
3 tablespoons margarine, softened	1 cup flour
1/2 cup milk	1 cup sugar
	1 tablespoon cornstarch
	1 cup boiling water

Spray 9" x 9" baking dish with non-stick cooking spray. In bottom of pan arrange fruit. Cream together 1/2 cup sugar and margarine. Add milk, baking powder, salt, and flour, and mix. Pour this dough mixture over fruit. Mix 1 cup sugar with cornstarch and sprinkle over dough. Pour boiling water over all. Place baking dish on cookie sheet and bake at 350° for 30 to 45 minutes. May be served warm or cold. Makes 6 - 8 servings.

FLUFFY OVEN EGGS AND BACON

1/2 pound bacon (about 12 slices)	1 1/4 cups milk
1/2 cup chopped onion	1/4 teaspoon salt
1/2 cup Bisquick mix	1/8 teaspoon pepper
3 eggs	1/2 cup shredded Cheddar or Swiss cheese

Spray 1 1/2 quart casserole with non-stick spray. Cut bacon slices into thirds. Cook and stir bacon in skillet over medium heat until almost crisp. Add onion. Cook, stirring frequently, until bacon is crisp. Drain. Spread bacon and onion in bottom of casserole. Beat Bisquick, eggs, milk, salt, and pepper until almost smooth. Slowly pour egg mixture over bacon; sprinkle with cheese. Bake at 375°, uncovered, until knife inserted in center comes out clean, approximately 35 minutes. *May substitute mushrooms for bacon. Makes 4 - 6 servings.

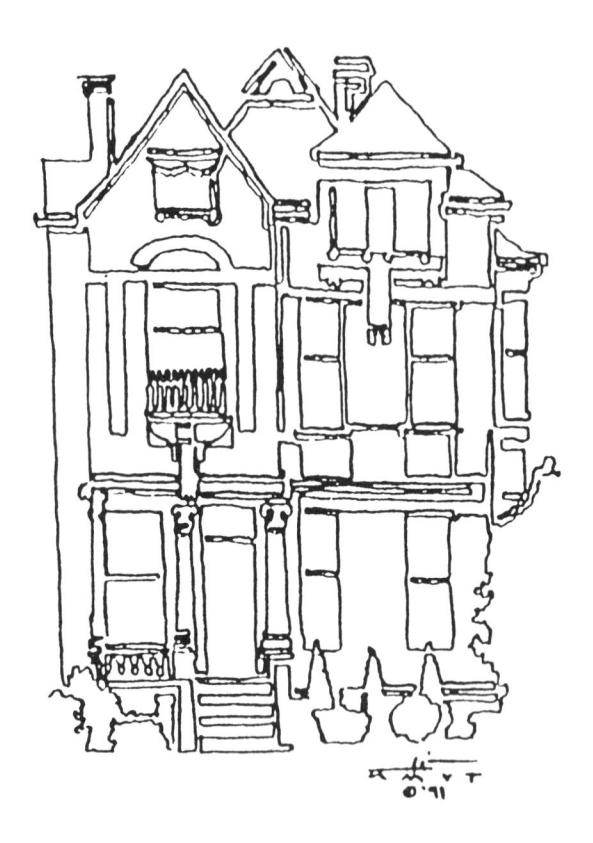

Rose Blossom Bed & Breakfast

1353 South Fourth • Louisville, KY 40208
502-636-0295
Innkeeper: Mary Ohlmann

The house, built in 1884, has been completely renovated, and there is much leaded glass throughout. Located in Old Louisville, surrounded by beautiful old buildings. On the National Historic Register. Park across the street. Many things to do and see within walking distance. Nice back porch with rockers, courtyard with pond. Seven lovely bedrooms. A good place to relax and be comfortable.

Rates: $$$ Includes full breakfast. Children over age 12 are welcome. No pets or smoking, please. We accept MasterCard, Visa, Am Ex, and Discover.

Recipes From Rose Blossom Bed & Breakfast

BREAKFAST IN ONE DISH

1 package hash browns
1 pound sausage, cooked & crumbled
1 pkg. shredded cheese, sharp or mild
1 onion, minced
Salt & pepper, to taste
3 tablespoons butter
12 eggs, beaten
1 cup milk

Layer hash browns, cooked sausage, cheese, onion, salt, and pepper in 9" x 13" casserole. Melt butter. Pour over the top. Beat eggs and milk, and pour evenly over casserole. Bake at 350° for about 45 to 60 minutes. Makes 10 servings.

PEAR SALAD

1 large can pears, drained (pieces or halves)
8 ounces cream cheese
3 ounce box lemon Jello
1 envelope Dream Whip

Drain pears, reserve 1 cup juice. Use electric mixer to cream pears and cream cheese. Heat pear juice and add Jello. Refrigerate until cool and slightly set. Mix Dream Whip according to directions on package. Mix all ingredients together. Pour into dish. Refrigerate until set. Can be kept in refrigerator for several days. Good as a salad for lunch or dinner, or served for breakfast instead of fresh fruit.

Rosedale Bed & Breakfast

1917 Cypress Street • Paris, KY 40361
606-987-1845   800-644-1862
Innkeepers: Katie and Jim Haag

Rosedale, a Kentucky Historic Site, invites you to enjoy its three secluded acres filled with lovely gardens, benches, a hammock, and lawn games. The 14-room Italianate brick home, built in 1862, is filled with antiques typical of that period. The cozy mahogany paneled library is but one of the many spots where guests can relax and enjoy their stay. Four guest rooms, family suites and private baths available. A delicious breakfast of seasonal favorites, complemented by homebaked breads, pastries, and muffins, make waking up in Bluegrass country a pleasure. The surrounding Bluegrass thoroughbred horse country provides the perfect pastoral approach to an area known for its social graces and warm country charm. Just 15 minutes from I-64, I-75, and the Kentucky Horse Park; and 20 to 30 minutes from Lexington, University of Kentucky, Rupp Arena, Red Mile, and Keeneland Race Courses. Antique lovers will certainly enjoy shopping in Paris and surrounding areas.

Rates: $$ - $$$ Includes full breakfast. Children over age 12 are welcome. No pets, please, but kennel nearby. Restricted smoking. We accept MasterCard and Visa.

Recipes From Rosedale Bed & Breakfast

APPLE TORTE

1/2 cup margarine
1/3 cup sugar
1/4 teaspoon vanilla
1 cup flour
8 ounces cream cheese
1/4 cup sugar
1 egg

1/2 teaspoon vanilla
4 cups peeled & thinly sliced cooking apples
1/3 cup sugar
1/2 teaspoon cinnamon
1/4 cup sliced almonds

Combine margarine, 1/3 cup sugar, 1/4 teaspoon vanilla, and flour. Press into bottom and sides of 10" deep-dish pie pan. Mix together cream cheese, 1/4 cup sugar, egg, and 1/2 teaspoon vanilla well. Pour into pan over pastry. Toss apples, 1/3 cup sugar, and cinnamon. Spoon over cream cheese mixture. Sprinkle almonds on top. Bake at 400° for 10 minutes, and at 350° for 25 minutes more. Allow to cool before cutting. Makes 8 servings.

APRICOT NUT BREAD

1/4 cup dried apricots
2 - 3 ounce pkgs. cream cheese
1/3 cup sugar
1 tablespoon flour
1 egg, beaten

1 box Pillsbury Nut Bread mix
1 egg, beaten
1/2 cup orange juice
1/2 cup water

Chop apricots and soften in small amount of water. Mix together cream cheese, sugar, flour, and 1 beaten egg. Set aside. In another bowl combine apricots, nut bread mix, 1 beaten egg, orange juice, and water. Pour 2/3 batter in greased loaf pan. Pour cheese mixture over the top and cover with rest of batter. Bake at 350° for one hour. Makes 1 loaf.

FRESH FRUIT WITH STRAWBERRY SAUCE

1 cup fresh strawberries
2 teaspoons sugar
1/4 teaspoon grated orange rind

Purée strawberries with sugar and orange rind. Chill until ready to use. Serve over orange sections and kiwi slices, with a garnish of fresh mint, if available.

ROSEDALE BLUEBERRY-PEACH SYRUP

1/2 cup sugar
1 teaspoon cinnamon
1/4 teaspoon allspice
1 teaspoon cornstarch
1/4 cup water
1 cup fresh or frozen blueberries
3/4 cup fresh or frozen sliced peaches

Combine sugar, cinnamon, allspice, cornstarch, and water. Bring to a boil and add blueberries and peaches. Reduce heat and simmer 10 to 15 minutes. Makes 2 cups of syrup.

Recipes From Rosedale Bed & Breakfast

ROSEDALE SCALLOPED PINEAPPLE

20 ounce can pineapple tidbits, drained	12 - 15 crushed Ritz crackers
3 tablespoons flour	1/4 cup melted butter or margarine
1/3 cup sugar	
1 cup shredded Cheddar cheese	

Drain pineapple, reserving 3 tablespoons juice. Combine pineapple juice, flour, and sugar. Add pineapple tidbits and cheese and mix well. Mix together cracker crumbs and melted butter. Pour pineapple mixture in shallow baking dish and top with crumb mixture. Bake at 350° for 30 minutes. Makes 8 servings.

WHIPPING CREAM BISCUITS

1 3/4 cups self-rising flour	1/2 pint whipping cream

Preheat oven to 450°. Measure flour into medium mixing bowl. Make well in center and add whipping cream. Blend with fork until mixture forms a ball. Roll on floured board to 1/4" thickness and cut out biscuits with small biscuit-cutter. Bake for 10 to 12 minutes. Makes 12 biscuits.

Sandford House Bed & Breakfast

1026 Russell Street • Covington, KY 41011
606-291-9133
Innkeepers: Dan and Linda Carter

Enjoy a leisurely delicious breakfast in an 1820's Federal, but redesigned in Second Empire style, mansion located in Seminary Square. Weather permitting, breakfast is served in award winning garden in our gazebo. Casual yet elegant, located 10 minutes from Cincinnati, 20 minutes from airport. Also, penthouse and carriage house are available for extended stay. Guest areas include queen size bedroom; garden suite with whirlpool tub; penthouse with beautiful view of Cincinnati; carriage house - fully furnished house with two bedrooms, and two bathrooms. All have private entrance and cable television.

Rates: $ - $$$$ Includes full breakfast. Children are welcome. Pets allowed. Restricted smoking. We accept MasterCard and Visa.

Recipes From Sandford House Bed & Breakfast

BACON CASSEROLE

2 cups plain croutons
1 1/2 cups shredded
　cheese
6 eggs
1/4 teaspoon dry mustard
1/4 teaspoon pepper

2 cups milk
1/2 teaspoon salt (opt.)
1/4 teaspoon onion
　powder
1/2 - 1 pound bacon,
　fried & crumbled

Preheat oven to 350°. Spray 9" x 13" casserole dish with Pam. Spread croutons evenly across bottom of dish. Sprinkle cheese evenly over croutons. In large bowl mix together all remaining ingredients except bacon. Pour slowly over croutons and cheese. Sprinkle crumbled bacon evenly on top of casserole. Bake 25 to 30 minutes. Let stand 5 minutes before serving. Makes 4 servings.

SAUSAGE SCRAMBLE

1 pound sausage
12 eggs
1 1/3 cups milk
1 teaspoon salt (opt.)

2 cups garlic and onion
　seasoned croutons
2 cups shredded sharp
　Cheddar cheese

Cook and stir sausage until light brown, and drain if needed. Place sausage in greased 9" x 13" baking dish. Beat eggs, milk, and salt (if desired); stir in croutons. Pour egg mixture over sausage. Sprinkle with cheese. Bake uncovered at 350° for 50 to 55 minutes, until knife inserted in center comes out clean. Let stand 5 minutes before serving. Garnish with tomato slices.

Sandusky House & O'Neal Log Cabin

1626 Delaney Ferry Road • Nicholasville, KY 40356
606-223-4730
Innkeepers: Jim and Linda Humphrey

Our tree-lined drive is just a prelude to a wonderful Bluegrass visit. A quiet 10-acre country setting amid horse farms, yet close to downtown Lexington and other attractions. The original 1780 land grant was given to Revolutionary War soldier Jacob Sandusky by Patrick Henry. Another soldier, George O'Neal, a Virginia scout and sharpshooter, built the Log Cabin in 1820. The Humphrey's lovingly reconstructed the Cabin in 1994. Brochures available.

Rates: $$ - $$$ Includes full breakfast. Children over age 12 are welcome in house. Children of all ages are welcome in cabin. No pets, please. Restricted smoking. We accept MasterCard and Visa.

COUNTRY QUICHE

1 deep dish 9" baked pie shell
4 ounces coarsely grated Swiss cheese
4 ounces coarsely grated sharp Cheddar cheese
3 eggs, beaten
1 cup heavy cream
1/4 teaspoon white pepper
1/4 teaspoon nutmeg
Paprika, to taste

Arrange the cheeses in baked pie shell. In saucepan heat eggs, cream, pepper, and nutmeg, stirring constantly until hot. Pour egg mixture over cheeses, stirring to mix evenly. Sprinkle with paprika. Bake at 350° for 30 minutes or until a knife inserted in center comes out clean. Cool for 5 to 10 minutes. *Ham bits, bacon, or diced vegetables can be added to the cheeses. Makes 6 - 8 servings.

CHOCOLATE ZUCCHINI BREAD

3 1/2 cups flour
2 teaspoons baking soda
1 1/2 teaspoons salt
1 teaspoon cinnamon
1/2 cup cocoa
3 cups sugar
2 cups grated zucchini
1/2 cup chopped walnuts
1 teaspoon vanilla
1 cup oil
2/3 cup water
4 eggs, beaten

Combine all dry ingredients. In separate bowl combine vanilla, oil, water, and eggs. Mix well. Add wet ingredients to dry ingredients. Mix only until all are blended. Bake in greased loaf pans at 325° for one hour or until tester comes out clean.

Recipes From Sandusky House & O'Neal Log Cabin

FRESH FRUIT WITH ALMOND SYRUP

2 cups water
1 1/2 cups sugar
3 tablespoons lemon juice
1/8 teaspoon salt
1/2 teaspoon almond extract
2 peaches, peeled & sliced
2 oranges, peeled & sectioned
2 kiwi fruits, peeled & sliced
3 plums, pitted & cut into wedges
1 medium pineapple, peeled & cut into chunks
1 honeydew melon, peeled & cut into chunks
1 cantaloupe, peeled & cut into chunks
1 1/2 cups seedless grapes, halved

In saucepan, combine water, sugar, lemon juice, and salt. Bring to boil. Reduce heat, boil gently about 20 minutes. Cool. Stir in almond extract. In large bowl combine fruits. Pour syrup over fruit; toss to combine. Cover and chill several hours. Makes 12 servings.

FRESH FRUIT WITH VANILLA YOGURT SAUCE

3 ounces light cream cheese
1/3 cup packed brown sugar
1/2 teaspoon vanilla
1 cup plain nonfat yogurt
8 cups assorted fresh fruit, cut into pieces
Toasted nuts or coconut (opt.)

In small mixer bowl combine cream cheese, brown sugar, and vanilla. Beat with electric mixer on medium speed until fluffy. Add yogurt; beat until smooth. Spoon sauce over assorted fresh fruit. If desired, top with nuts or coconut. Makes 8 servings.

Recipes From Sandusky House & O'Neal Log Cabin

MAKE-AHEAD BREAKFAST EGGS

12 eggs
1/2 cup milk
1/2 teaspoon salt
1/4 teaspoon pepper
1 tablespoon butter

8 ounces sour cream
12 slices bacon, cooked
 & crumbled
1 cup shredded sharp
 Cheddar cheese

In medium bowl, beat eggs; stir in milk, salt, and pepper. Set aside. In large skillet, over medium-low heat, melt butter. Pour in egg mixture. Cook, stirring occasionally, until eggs are set but still moist; remove from heat to cool. Stir in sour cream. Spread evenly into buttered 2-quart shallow baking dish (12" x 7"). Top with bacon and cheese. Cover with aluminum foil and refrigerate overnight. Preheat oven to 300°. Uncover eggs, bake for 15 to 20 minutes, or until hot and cheese has melted. Makes 8 - 10 servings.

PEAR MUFFINS

2 cups flour
1/2 cup brown sugar
1 teaspoon baking
 soda
1/2 teaspoon salt
2 teaspoons ginger
1/8 teaspoon cloves
1/8 teaspoon nutmeg

1 cup plain yogurt
1/2 cup oil
3 tablespoons molasses
1 egg, beaten
1 1/2 cups diced ripe
 pears, unpeeled
1/2 cup raisins
1/2 cup chopped nuts

Grease 12 large muffin cups. In large bowl mix the first 7 ingredients. In medium bowl combine yogurt, oil, molasses, and egg. Blend well. Fold wet ingredients into dry ingredients and mix until just blended. Add pears, raisins, and nuts. Spoon batter into prepared muffin cups. Bake at 400° for 20 minutes. Makes 12 muffins.

Seldon Renaker Inn

24 South Walnut Street • Cynthiana, KY 41031
606-234-3752
Innkeepers: Jim and Juanita Ingram

The Seldon Renaker Inn was built in 1885 as a private residence by Seldon Renaker for his growing family. Centrally located in downtown Cynthiana, within walking distance of the museum, restored movie house, fine dining and historical landmarks. Travelers are invited to stay in one of six guest rooms, all with private baths. 3 efficiency units available. Each room is beautifully decorated with an eclectic mixture of antiques and traditional furnishings. The large hallways, high ceilings, and front porch swing are reminiscent of another era; whereas, air conditioning and cable television remind us of today's requirements for comfortable living. A continental plus breakfast is served daily in the parlor. Fitness room available. On site antique shop and tea room.

Rates: $ - $$ Includes continental plus breakfast. Children are welcome. No pets, please. Restricted smoking. We accept MasterCard and Visa.

Recipes From Seldon Renaker Inn

LEMON CREAM TEA CAKES

1 cup butter
1 1/4 cups sugar
2 eggs
1 teaspoon lemon extract
2 1/2 cups cake flour
1/2 teaspoon salt
1/2 teaspoon baking soda

Cream butter and sugar. Mix eggs in one at a time; add lemon extract. Sift dry ingredients and add to mixture. Refrigerate overnight. Roll out on floured board and cut out. Bake at 350° for 8 to 10 minutes.

OATMEAL CHOCOLATE CHIP MUFFINS

1 1/4 cups quick-cooking oats
1 1/4 cups milk
1 egg
1/2 cup oil
3/4 cup firmly packed brown sugar, divided
1 cup pecans, divided
3/4 cup semi-sweet chocolate chips
1 1/4 cups all-purpose flour
4 teaspoons baking powder
1 teaspoon salt

Combine oats and milk, allow to stand 15 minutes. Preheat oven to 400°. Stir egg, oil, 1/2 cup brown sugar, 1/2 cup pecans, and chocolate chips into oat mixture. In large bowl, combine flour, baking powder, and salt. Add oat mixture to flour mixture, stirring just until all dry ingredients are moistened. Fill each cup of a greased 12-cup muffin tin 2/3 full with batter. Sprinkle tops with remaining brown sugar and pecans. Bake 20 to 25 minutes or until the top of a muffin springs back when lightly touched. Makes 12 muffins.

Sills Inn Bed & Breakfast

270 Montgomery Avenue • Versailles, KY 40383
606-873-4478   800-526-9801
Innkeepers: Tony Sills and Glenn Blind

The restored Victorian Inn, located in historic downtown Versailles, is just 7 minutes west of the Lexington Airport & the famous Keeneland Race Course. Near the state capital, the beautiful Bluegrass thoroughbred horse farm region, and the restored Shaker Village. Short walk to antique shops, art studios, cafes, and quaint restaurants. Twelve guest rooms, individually decorated, each with private bath and king or queen size bed. Nine suites have jacuzzis for two. Complimentary snacks are available for the weary traveler, plus a menu book of recommended restaurants in the area. Full gourmet breakfast served on the Sun Porch on china, crystal, and linen. The business traveler's room contains a well-lit desk, 2-line phone jack with modem hook-up, and private phone. Access to FAX machine, copier, airport transportation, and meeting room. Within minutes of local businesses and a short drive to Lexington or Frankfort. Enjoy Southern hospitality at its fullest.

Rates: $$ - $$$$ Includes full breakfast. Limited accommodations for children - extra person charge. No pets or smoking, please. We accept MasterCard, Visa, Am Ex, Discover, and Diners Club.

Recipes From Sills Inn Bed & Breakfast

BAKED FRENCH TOAST

1 1/2 Hawaiian rolls or dinner rolls, broken into small pieces
3 eggs
1/4 cup milk
1/8 cup pancake syrup

Break rolls into small pieces and place in bottom of well-sprayed ramekin dish. Mix together eggs, milk and syrup. Pour over bread and stir to moisten. Place ramekin on sheet of foil, pull top up over the dish, making a tent. *May layer bottom of dish with frozen or fresh fruit before adding bread. May be made the night before and refrigerated. Bake at 375° for one hour. Makes 1 serving.

SPINACH SOUFFLÉ

1 - 10 ounce pkg. frozen chopped spinach
24 eggs
8 ounces cream cheese, softened
2 teaspoons garlic powder
1 teaspoon salt
16 dashes hot sauce
Dash of pepper
2 cups Monterey Jack cheese, grated
Fresh tomato slices (opt.)

Microwave spinach on high for 7 minutes and set aside. Mix next six ingredients well with mixer. Add cheese, and mix well. Add cooked spinach. Pour 1 cup of mixture into each of 8 individual well-sprayed round ramekins. Bake at 375° for 30 to 35 minutes. Serve immediately. Top with fresh tomato slices before serving, if desired. *Mixture may be refrigerated for 3 to 4 days. Makes 8 servings.

Silver Cliff Inn Bed & Breakfast

1980 Lake Barkley Drive - Hwy. 295 • Old Kuttawa, KY 42055
502-388-5858
Innkeepers: Anne-Marie and Jack Ireland

Silver Cliff Inn, a 5,000 square foot Victorian mansion (circa 1874), located on beautiful Lake Barkley has six bedrooms (including two suites with private baths), seven fireplaces, central heat and air, is open year round (except Christmas & Thanksgiving). It is across the street from beach and park, 1/2 block from Kuttawa Harbor Marina and Seaplane Base, 9 miles from Patti's 1880's Restaurant, recently named one of the best restaurants by <u>Southern Living</u> magazine; several PGA-rated golf courses nearby; just off Western Kentucky Parkway and I-24. A full country gourmet breakfast is served to guests by fireplace or on the veranda; catered brunch, lunch or dinner. Dessert served in the evening. Refrigerator stocked for late night snacks. Entire house can be reserved for private family reunions, corporate functions, etc. Reservations (and deposit) required.

Rates: $$$ Includes full breakfast. Children over age 10 are welcome. (Exceptions if well-behaved). No pets, please. Restricted smoking.

Recipes From Silver Cliff Inn Bed & Breakfast

BREAKFAST ENCHILADAS

8 medium-sized flour tortillas
4 ounce can green chilies, diced
2 - 10 1/2 ounce cans cream of mushroom soup
1 pint sour cream
1 pound Monterey Jack cheese, shredded
12 eggs, lightly scrambled
4 ounce can sliced black olives

Mix chilies, soup, sour cream, and half of cheese together. Divide mixture in half. To one half of mixture, add cooked eggs. Divide mixture evenly among tortillas and place in 9" x 13" greased baking pan. Cover tortillas with remaining half of mixture and top with remaining cheese and olives. Bake at 350° for 15 minutes or until well heated through. Makes 6 - 8 servings.

EGGS MORNAY

8 hard-boiled eggs
1/2 cup green peas
1/4 teaspoon curry powder
1/4 teaspoon salt
1/4 teaspoon red pepper
1/4 teaspoon celery salt
1/4 cup parsley, chopped
1/4 cup onion, chopped
2 tablespoons half and half
1 1/2 tablespoons butter
1 1/2 tablespoons flour
1 1/2 cups milk
Sharp cheese, grated
Ground cooked ham

Hard boil eggs. Remove yolks. Mash yolks, and blend in green peas, curry powder, salt, red pepper, and celery salt. Add parsley, onion, and half and half. Refill egg whites with yolk mixture and place in casserole. For cream sauce: Melt butter in saucepan, add flour. Add milk all at once, and cook for one minute. Cover eggs with cream sauce and sprinkle the top with cheese and ham. Heat about 10 minutes at 450°. Makes 8 servings.

Susan B. Seay's Magnolia Manor

401 South Seventh • Mayfield, KY 42066
502-247-4108
Innkeeper: Susan B. Seay

Circa 1900 Greek Revival, located 2 blocks from downtown Mayfield. Thirteen room gracious home restored to its original beauty and splendor, featuring majestic ceilings, hardwood floors, and a staircase you'd expect Scarlet O'Hara to descend. Master bedroom downstairs has private bath, while three guest rooms upstairs share two baths. Distinctive decor and antique furnishings are your surroundings while "Graves County charm and hospitality" are the main amenities offered my guests while you "rest and reminisce." Convenient location to American Quilt Museum, Paducah & Land Between The Lakes, or enjoy the quaint charm of our lovely city, its antique stores and championship croquet courts. The home has hosted lovely weddings, receptions, parties and dinners with catering offered by Sisters Catering, or business meetings and seminars welcome the ambiance of **Magnolia Manor**.

Rates: $$ Includes continental plus breakfast. Children are welcome. No pets, please. Restricted smoking.

Recipes From Susan B. Seay's Magnolia Manor

APPLE DANISH BARS

3 cups sifted flour
1 teaspoon salt
1 cup shortening
1 egg, separated
Milk as needed
1 cup crushed Corn Flakes cereal
8 large apples, pared & sliced (8 cups)
1 cup sugar
1 teaspoon ground cinnamon
Warm water to moisten edges of dough
1 cup sifted confectioners sugar
3 tablespoons water
1 teaspoon vanilla

Sift together flour and salt into bowl. Cut in shortening until crumbly. Add enough milk to beaten egg yolk to make 1/2 cup liquid. Add to flour mixture, mix until moist. Divide dough almost in half. Roll out larger half; place in 15 1/2" x 10 1/2" x 1" jellyroll pan. Press onto sides of pan. Sprinkle with crushed Corn Flakes. Arrange apple slices over cereal. Combine sugar and cinnamon, sprinkle over apples. Roll out other half of dough to fit top. Make vents in top. Moisten edges of dough with warm water; seal. Spread stiffly beaten egg white over crust. Bake at 375° for one hour or until golden. Combine confectioners sugar, water, and vanilla, mix well. Spread on bars while warm. Makes 12 servings.

CHOCOLATE BISCUIT PUDDING

2 - 2 1/2 dozen biscuits, or 1 loaf white bread
1/2 stick butter
2 eggs, beaten well
2 tablespoons cocoa
1 1/2 cups sugar
1 1/2 - 2 cups milk

Crumble biscuits or bread. Add butter, eggs, cocoa, and sugar. Stir a little. Add enough milk to make mixture of pouring consistency. Mash well with potato masher. Pour into greased or sprayed large iron skillet. Bake at 350° for one hour. May also be baked in mini-muffin tins, about 15 minutes. Serve hot.

Trinity Hills Farm Bed & Breakfast Home

10455 Old Lovelaceville Road • Paducah, KY 42001
502-488-3999   800-488-3998
Innkeepers: The Driver Family

17-acre country retreat ideal for romantic getaways and family gatherings. Guests enjoy fishing, birding at its best, paddleboating, picnics, hiking, farm animals, peacocks, water gardens, and relaxing in one of the spas or hammock. Our new 3-story home designed specifically to meet various needs of our guests features four uniquely decorated guest rooms with private baths and robes (2 rooms with private entrances and 2 suites with spa or whirlpool), handicapped accessibility, unique stained glass projects, fireplaces, vaulted ceilings, and TV/Game/Exercise room. We feature evening desserts and full country or gourmet breakfast. Our family is committed to providing exceptional bed & breakfast services to insure each guest a memorable and enjoyable visit.

Rates: $$ - $$$ Includes full breakfast. Children are welcome. Pets allowed with prior notice. Restricted smoking. We accept MasterCard, Visa, and Discover.

Recipes From Trinity Hills F...

BACON-SAUSAGE BREAKF...

5 slices bacon, cooked
4 sausage patties, cooked
6 slices bread, torn into small pieces (or leftover buns & biscuits)
1 can sliced mushrooms

1 cup grate...
6 eggs
2 cups...
1 teaspo...(opt.)
Salt & pepper, to taste

Grease a 9" x 13" baking dish or 2 - 9" round Pyrex pie plates. Cook bacon and sausage; drain and crumble. (*We microwave bacon while sausage browns.) In baking dish, layer bread, bacon, sausage, mushrooms, and cheese. Beat eggs. Add milk and dry mustard; add salt, and pepper to taste. Beat well and pour over layers. Bake at 350° for 40 to 45 minutes or 25 minutes for quiches. *May be refrigerated overnight before cooking or after cooking.

SOUR CREAM/HASH BROWN CASSEROLE

2 pounds frozen shredded hash brown potatoes, thawed
1/2 cup margarine, melted
1 teaspoon salt
1/2 teaspoon black pepper
1 can cream of celery soup

1 - 2 tablespoons minced dry onions
1 pint sour cream
1/4 cup salad dressing
1 cup cheese, grated (half Cheddar, half Colby Jack cheese)

Topping:
2 cups crushed Corn Flakes cereal

2 - 3 tablespoons melted margarine

Combine hash browns, margarine, salt, black pepper, soup, onions, sour cream, salad dressing, and cheese. Pour into greased 9" x 13" casserole dish. Bake at 350° for about 30 minutes. Combine topping ingredients and spread over filling mixture. Bake an additional 30 minutes.

Victorian House Bed & Breakfast

130 North Main Street - P.O. Box 104 • Smith's Grove, KY 42171
502-563-9403
Innkeepers: Velma and Bill Crist

Victorian House Bed & Breakfast was built in 1875. It is 3-bricks thick, and is located in the center of historical Smith's Grove, Kentucky. There are four large, lovely guest bedrooms, all with private baths. A tray with coffee, juice, and hot muffins is served in rooms at 7:00 A.M. Full country breakfast is served in the formal dining room at 8:00 A.M. Relax in two lovely parlors or on wraparound porch. Stroll around the two acres of lovely grounds and visit the many antique shops. Nearby are many areas of interest, including Mammoth Cave, Corvette Museum, Shakertown, and the Capitol Arts Theater, to name a few.

Rates: $$$ Includes full breakfast. No pets, please. Restricted smoking. We accept MasterCard, Visa, and Am Ex.

Recipes From Victorian House Bed & Breakfast

HASH BROWN CASSEROLE

3 tablespoons oil	1 red pepper, chopped
2 pounds frozen hash brown potatoes	2 cups cubed ham
	10 eggs, beaten
1 onion, chopped	Salt & pepper, to taste
1 green pepper, chopped	1 1/2 cups Cheddar cheese, shredded

Heat oil in large skillet. Add hash browns, onion, and bell peppers. Cook until potatoes begin to brown. Spray 9" x 13" baking dish with Pam. Spread potato mixture in pan. Top with ham. Pour beaten eggs over all and season to taste with salt and pepper. Gently stir to coat all ingredients with eggs. Sprinkle with cheese. Refrigerate overnight. Bake uncovered at 375° for 35 minutes. Makes 8 servings.

PEACH DELIGHT

2 - 20 ounce cans peach halves	1/2 cup oatmeal
	1/2 cup granola
1 cup brown sugar	1/2 cup melted butter
1/2 cup chopped pecans	1 cup vanilla yogurt

Preheat broiler to 500°. Combine 1/2 cup brown sugar, pecans, oatmeal, granola, and melted butter. Mix well, set aside. Arrange a layer of peaches (rounded sides down) in shallow baking dish. Using remaining 1/2 cup brown sugar, place 1/2 teaspoon of sugar in center of each peach half. Broil 5 minutes or until brown sugar is melted. Remove from broiler and place a heaping spoonful of topping in center of each peach. Place under broiler again, for about 1 minute. Be careful not to burn! Remove from broiler and top each peach with a tablespoon of yogurt. Serve warm - enjoy! Makes 8 - 10 servings.

The Wayfarer

1240 Old Mammoth Cave Road • Cave City, KY 42127
502-773-3366
Innkeepers: Larry and Becky Bull

The Wayfarer is conveniently located at the boundary line of Mammoth Cave National Park, five miles from Cave City. A restored 1930's souvenir shop, currently a Kentucky craft gift shop, Floyd Collins Museum, and recently opened B&B. Stay in one of five guest rooms complete with private baths and decorated to suit everyone. A complete country ham breakfast served before leaving to tour Mammoth Cave.

Rates: $$ Includes full breakfast. Children are welcome. No pets or smoking, please. We accept MasterCard, Visa, Am Ex, and Discover.

FRENCH TOAST WITH ALMONDS

1 pound loaf unsliced white or raisin bread	1 tablespoon almond extract
8 eggs	1/2 teaspoon cinnamon
3 cups milk	Dash of nutmeg
1/4 cup sugar	1/2 cup sliced almonds

Prepare in advance. Slice bread into 6 - 1" slices and arrange in buttered 9" x 13" baking pan. Beat eggs with milk, sugar, almond extract, and cinnamon. Pour over bread. Sprinkle with nutmeg and almonds. Refrigerate covered for 4 hours or overnight. Bake uncovered at 350° for 45 to 60 minutes. Makes 4 - 6 servings.

HASH BROWN PIE

24 ounces frozen hash brown potatoes, thawed	1 cup shredded Monterey Jack cheese
1/3 cup butter, melted	1/2 cup cream or milk
1 cup diced ham	2 eggs
1 cup shredded Cheddar cheese	1/4 teaspoon salt
	1/4 teaspoon pepper

Spread thawed potatoes on paper towels to absorb moisture. Preheat oven to 425°. Butter a 9" pie plate. Make a crust of potatoes by pressing them firmly along the bottom and sides of pie plate. Brush with melted butter. Bake for 20 minutes. Reduce heat to 350°. Combine ham and cheeses. Turn out onto crust. Beat cream, eggs, salt, and pepper, and pour over ham and cheeses. Bake 30 to 40 minutes. Makes 6 servings.

Weller Haus Bed & Breakfast

319 Poplar Street • Bellevue, KY 41073
606-431-6829   800-431-4287
Innkeepers: Mary and Vernon Weller

Savor the charm of the 1880's tucked away in one of the five antique-appointed guest rooms of the **Weller Haus** in the Historic Kentucky River District of Bellevue, Kentucky. Five minutes from downtown Cincinnati, Ohio, this "Preservation Awarded" Inn offers a relaxing small town atmosphere of church steeples, tree-lined city streets, and Victorian rooftops. Choose from 5 accommodations to secure your comfort - all with private baths, one with jacuzzi for two. Coffees, teas, soft drinks, and pretzels are complimentary fare for guests, either in the ivy-covered gathering kitchen or cathedral ceiling great room with adjoining secluded garden. Return to the casual elegance of a bygone era in our presentation of an exquisite breakfast of selected hot entrees, fruit, homemade muffins, breads, and coffee cakes, served amid the patterned glass, linens, laces, and porcelains of yesteryear. In our sixth year, we graciously extend memorable hospitality and a most kindly welcome.

Rates: $$$ - $$$$ Includes full breakfast. Children are welcome. No pets, please. Restricted smoking. We accept MasterCard and Visa.

Recipes From Weller Haus Bed & Breakfast

ENGLISH MUFFIN BREAD

5 - 6 cups flour
1/2 cup raisins
2 packets active dry yeast
1 tablespoon sugar
2 teaspoons salt
1 1/2 teaspoons cinnamon
1/4 teaspoon baking soda
2 cups milk
1/2 cup water
Cornmeal

In bowl combine 3 cups flour, raisins, yeast, sugar, salt, cinnamon, and baking soda. Combine milk and water in pan and heat until liquids are very warm (120° - 130°). Add to dry ingredients and beat well. Stir in remaining flour to make a stiff dough. Spoon into 2 - 9" x 5" x 3" loaf pans which have been greased and coated with cornmeal. Sprinkle tops of loaves with additional cornmeal. Cover with towel. Let rise in warm place, free from draft, for 45 minutes. Bake at 400° for 25 minutes. Remove from pans immediately and cool. Slice and toast. Makes 2 loaves.

FRENCH BREAKFAST MUFFINS

1/3 cup margarine
1/2 cup sugar
1 egg
1 1/2 cups flour
1 1/2 teaspoons baking powder
1/2 teaspoon salt
1/4 teaspoon nutmeg
1/2 cup milk
<u>Topping</u>:
1/3 cup sugar
1 teaspoon cinnamon
1/2 cup butter, melted
   (no substitutes)

Mix margarine, sugar, and egg. Mix dry ingredients, then mix alternately with milk into egg mixture. Grease muffin cups with non-stick spray. Fill muffin cups 2/3 full (do not use muffin papers). Bake at 350° for 15 to 20 minutes. For topping: Mix sugar, cinnamon and melted butter. Brush muffin tops with this mixture as soon as they are out of the oven. Makes 9 - 12 muffins.

Willis Graves 1830's Bed & Breakfast Inn

5825 Jefferson Street • Burlington, KY 41005
606-344-0665   606-689-5096
Innkeepers: Bob and Jean Brames, Nancy and Bob Swartzel

Willis Graves served as clerk for Boone County during the 1810's and 1820's. He built what is now the B&B named for him in the early 1830's. The home is simple but elegant, with Flemish bond brickwork and federal mantels. Currently, we have one suite available with private bath, bedroom, and living room with fold-out couch. Guests enjoy the many period antiques and reproductions which furnish the suite. A country setting, private entrance, and off-street parking make for a relaxing stay. Our location in historic Burlington provides much interest. The Boone County fairgrounds is next door and hosts antique shows (seven per year), car and horse shows, a county fair, and bluegrass festivals. Around the bend are antique and craft shops. The Dinsmore Homestead and Rabbit Hash River community are nearby. We are only a highway's drive of 12 minutes to the International Airport, and 20 minutes to downtown Cincinnati, Ohio.

Rates: $$ Includes continental plus breakfast. Children over age 12 are welcome. No pets or smoking, please.

Recipes From Willis Graves 1830's B & B Inn

ORANGE POUND CAKE WITH BLUEBERRIES

1 cup cake flour
1 teaspoon baking powder
3/4 cup (1 1/2 sticks) unsalted butter, softened
1 cup sugar
3 large eggs
1 large egg yolk
1/3 cup orange juice
Zest of 2 oranges
2 cups plain yogurt
Sugar, to taste
4 ounces fresh blueberries

Preheat oven to 350°. Butter and flour loaf pan thoroughly. Set aside. Sift together cake flour and baking powder - set aside. Beat together butter and 1 cup sugar at medium speed until light and fluffy. Add the eggs and egg yolk, one at a time, until incorporated. Add orange juice, and zest, and beat until just mixed. Gently fold in flour mixture in 3 batches and pour batter into pan. Bake for 25 to 30 minutes or until cake springs back to a gentle touch. Carefully unmold and let cool on cake rack. To make Blueberry Yogurt: Mix yogurt, sugar, to taste, and blueberries. Serve one slice of cake with blueberry yogurt on the side. Makes 1 - 10" loaf pan.

WILLIS' YOGURT COFFEE CAKE

1/4 pound butter
1 cup sugar
2 eggs
1 pint plain yogurt
2 cups flour
1 teaspoon baking soda
1 teaspoon baking powder
4 tablespoons brown sugar
2 teaspoons cinnamon
1 cup chopped pecans

Cream together butter and sugar. Add eggs, yogurt, flour, baking soda, and baking powder, and mix thoroughly. Grease and flour tube pan. Spoon half of the mixture into pan - it will be thick. Mix brown sugar, cinnamon, and pecans and sprinkle half over batter in pan. Add remaining batter and top with remaining brown sugar mixture. Bake at 375° for 30 to 35 minutes. *At The Willis Graves Bed & Breakfast Inn, coffee cake is served with seasonal blush raspberries.

Woodhaven Bed & Breakfast

401 South Hubbards Lane • Louisville, KY 40207
502-895-1011   888-895-1011
Innkeeper: Marsha Burton

This beautiful Gothic Revival mansion, which was built in 1853 by Theodore Brown, incorporates distinctive features from a design by A. J. Downing. Elaborately carved woodwork, winding staircases, and spacious rooms, tastefully decorated with antiques, handcrafts, and a touch of whimsy, combine to create a truly special atmosphere. Each of the seven bedrooms offers private baths, some with whirlpools, televisions, telephones, clock radios, and complimentary coffee and tea stations. Reasonable rates include a full gourmet breakfast served from 7:30 A.M. to 9:30 A.M. in the formal dining room. Guests are invited to enjoy the antique-filled common areas with 14' ceilings, magnificent woodwork, and light streaming in floor-to-ceiling windows. Breakfast includes assorted pastries, fresh fruit, granola, and yogurts, fresh orange and grapefruit juice, jams, French toast, pancakes, breakfast pie, and homemade breads for toast.

Rates: $$ - $$$ Includes full breakfast. Children are welcome. No pets or smoking, please. We accept MasterCard and Visa.

Recipes From Woodhaven Bed & Breakfast

CARAMEL FRENCH TOAST

1 stick butter
1 cup brown sugar
2 tablespoons Karo Light corn syrup
1 loaf French bread, cut into 1" pieces
6 eggs
1 1/2 cups milk
2 teaspoons vanilla
Cinnamon to taste
Mixed berries & whipped cream

Combine butter, brown sugar, and Karo syrup in saucepan over medium heat until it boils. Pour into 9" x 13" casserole pan. Slice French bread into 1" pieces. Lay in pan over caramel. Mix eggs, milk, and vanilla, and pour over bread. Sprinkle cinnamon over top and bake at 300° for one hour. Serve with mixed berries and whipped cream. Makes 8 servings.

WOODHAVEN DILL BREAD

3 cups self-rising flour
3 tablespoons brown sugar
1 tablespoon dill
12 oz. can light beer
2 tablespoons butter, melted

Preheat oven to 375°. Mix flour, brown sugar, dill, and beer together in mixer. Pour into greased bread loaf pan. Pour melted butter over top of bread mixture. Bake for 50 minutes. Slice when cool - can be reheated later in foil wrap. Also is very good toasted with ham and a poached egg. Makes 8 - 10 slices.

More Bed & Breakfast Cookbooks

American Mornings - Favorite Breakfast Recipes From Bed & Breakfast Inns
Features breakfast recipes from 302 inns throughout the country, with complete information about each inn. 320 pgs. $12.95

State Association Cookbooks

What's Cooking Inn Arizona - A Recipe Guidebook of the AZ Assn. of B&B Inns
Features 126 recipes from 21 inns throughout the state of Arizona, with complete information about each inn. 96 pgs. $12.95

Pure Gold - Colorado Treasures / Recipes From B&B Innkeepers of Colorado
Features more than 100 recipes from 54 inns throughout the state of Colorado, with complete information about each inn. 96 pgs. $9.95

Colorado Columbine Delicacies - Recipes From B&B Innkeepers of Colorado
Features 115 recipes from 43 inns throughout the state of Colorado, with complete information about each inn. Features special lay-flat binding. 112 pgs. $10.95

Inn-describably Delicious - Recipes From The Illinois B&B Assn. Innkeepers
Features recipes from 82 inns throughout the state of Illinois, with complete information about each inn. 112 pgs. $9.95

The Indiana Bed & Breakfast Association Cookbook and Directory
Features recipes from 75 inns throughout the state of Indiana, with complete information about each inn. 96 pgs. $9.95

The Indiana Bed & Breakfast Association Cookbook 2
Features recipes from inns throughout the state of Indiana, with complete information about each inn. 128 pgs. $10.95

Savor the Inns of Kansas - Recipes From Kansas Bed & Breakfasts
Features recipes from 51 inns throughout the state of Kansas, with complete information about each inn. 112 pgs. $9.95

Sunrise in Kentucky
Features recipes from inns throughout the state of Kentucky, with complete information about each inn. 112 pgs. $9.95

Another Sunrise in Kentucky
Features recipes from inns throughout the state of Kentucky, with complete information about each inn. 112 pgs. $9.95

Just Inn Time for Breakfast (Michigan Lake To Lake B & B Association)
Features recipes from 93 inns throughout the state of Michigan, with complete information about each inn. Features special lay-flat binding. 128 pgs. $10.95

Be Our Guest - Cooking with Missouri's Innkeepers
Features recipes from 43 inns throughout the state of Missouri, with complete information about each inn. 96 pgs. $9.95

Palmetto Hospitality - Inn Style (South Carolina)
Features over 90 recipes from 47 inns throughout the state of South Carolina, with complete information about each inn. 112 pgs. $10.00

A Taste of Tennessee - Recipes From Tennessee Bed & Breakfast Inns
Features 80 recipes from 40 inns throughout the state of Tennessee, with complete information about each inn. 96 pgs. $9.95

Good Morning West Virginia! - Travel Guide & Recipe Collection
Features 119 recipes from inns throughout the state of West Virginia, with complete information about each inn, and travel information about the state. 160 pgs. $12.95

ORDER FORM

Indicate the quantity of the book(s) that you wish to order below. Please feel free to copy this form for your order. For information please call (812) 663-4948. MAIL THIS ORDER TO:

Winters Publishing
P.O. Box 501
Greensburg, IN 47240

Quantity

	Book	Price	
_____	*Heart Healthy Hospitality*	$10.95 each	_____
_____	*Mountain Mornings*	10.95 each	_____
_____	*American Mornings*	12.95 each	_____
_____	*What's Cooking Inn Arizona*	12.95 each	_____
_____	*Pure Gold - Colorado Treasures*	9.95 each	_____
_____	*Colorado Columbine Delicacies*	10.95 each	_____
_____	*Inn-describably Delicious*	9.95 each	_____
_____	*Indiana B&B Assn. Cookbook*	9.95 each	_____
_____	*Indiana B&B Assn. Cookbook 2*	10.95 each	_____
_____	*Savor the Inns of Kansas*	9.95 each	_____
_____	*Sunrise in Kentucky*	9.95 each	_____
_____	*Another Sunrise in Kentucky*	9.95 each	_____
_____	*Just Inn Time for Breakfast*	10.95 each	_____
_____	*Be Our Guest*	9.95 each	_____
_____	*Palmetto Hospitality - Inn Style*	10.00 each	_____
_____	*A Taste of Tennessee*	9.95 each	_____
_____	*Good Morning West Virginia*	12.95 each	_____
	Shipping Charge	2.00 each	_____
	5% Sales Tax (IN residents <u>ONLY</u>)		_____
		TOTAL	_____

Send to:

Name: _____

Address: _____

City: _____ State: _____ Zip: _____

Bed & Breakfast Cookbooks
from Individual Inns

Heart Healthy Hospitality - Low Fat Breakfast Recipes From The Manor At Taylor's Store Bed and Breakfast Country Inn
Features over 130 wonderful low-fat breakfast recipes from The Manor at Taylor's Store in Virginia. Features special lay-flat binding. 160 pgs. $10.95

Mountain Mornings - Breakfasts and other recipes from The Inn at 410 B&B
Features a variety of about 90 tempting recipes from The Inn at 410 B&B in Arizona. Features special lay-flat binding. 128 pgs. $10.95

INDEX OF BED & BREAKFASTS

AUGUSTA
  Augusta White House Inn B&B ...12
BARDSTOWN
  Beautiful Dreamer B&B 22
  Old Talbott Tavern/
    McLean House........................64
BELLEVUE
  Weller Haus B&B....................104
BOWLING GREEN
  Alpine Lodge............................10
BURLINGTON
  Willis Graves 1830's
    B&B Inn...............................106
CAVE CITY
  The Wayfarer..........................102
COVINGTON
  Licking Riverside
    Historic B&B 50
  Sandford House B&B 84
CYNTHIANA
  Seldon Renaker Inn....................90
DANVILLE
  Randolph House........................72
FRANKFORT
  Cedar Rock Farm 32
FRANKLIN
  College Street Inn 36
GEORGETOWN
  Bourbon House Farm 24
  Pineapple Inn B&B....................70
GHENT
  Ghent House B&B.....................38
HARRODSBURG
  Bauer Haus B&B 16
  Baxter House............................20
HENDERSON
  L & N Bed & Breakfast 46
LEBANON
  Myrtledene B&B 60
LEXINGTON
  A TRUE INN B&B 6
  The Brand House at
    Rose Hill...............................26

LOUISVILLE
  Aleksander House.......................8
  Inn at the Park B&B..................44
  Old Louisville Inn B&B............62
  Rocking Horse Manor B&B........76
  Rose Blossom B&B 78
  Woodhaven B&B 108
MARION
  Lafayette Heights
    Clubhouse..............................48
  Myers' B&B 58
MAYFIELD
  Susan B. Seay's
    Magnolia Manor.....................96
MIDDLESBORO
  The RidgeRunner B&B 74
NEW CASTLE
  The Oldham House B&B
    and Antiques 66
NICHOLASVILLE
  Cedar Haven Farm B&B.............28
  Sandusky House &
    O'Neal Log Cabin..................86
OLD KUTTAWA
  Silver Cliff Inn B&B.................94
OWENSBORO
  Helton House B&B 42
PARIS
  Rosedale B&B 80
PADUCAH
  Trinity Hills Farm B&B Home....98
RICHMOND
  Barnes Mill B&B 14
ROGERS
  Cliffview Resort........................34
SMITH'S GROVE
  Victorian House B&B 100
SOMERSET
  Osbornes of Cabin Hollow 68
SPRINGFIELD
  Glenmar Plantation B&B............40
  Maple Hill Manor B&B 52
STEARNS
  The Marcum-Porter
    House B&B 56
VERSAILLES
  Sills Inn B&B...........................92